Machine Learning with oneAPI

oneAPI is a unified programming model and software development kit (SDK) from Intel that empowers software developers to generate high-performance applications that can run on different devices, comprising CPUs, GPUs, FPGAs, and other accelerators. It lets developers write code once and deploy it on multiple architectures, decreasing the complexity as well as the cost and time of software development. One of the significant strengths of oneAPI is in its capability to support an eclectic range of devices and architectures, including artificial intelligence, high-performance computing, and data analytics. Along with libraries, tools, and compilers, oneAPI makes it cool for developers to create optimized code for an extensive variety of applications, making it an indispensable tool for any developer who wants to create high-performance software and reap the benefit of the latest hardware technologies. The versatility of oneAPI, by means of appropriate theory and practical implementation with the latest tools in machine learning, has been presented in a simple yet effective way in this book that caters to everyone's needs. Come on, let's unleash the true power of our code across varied architectures!

Machine Learning with oneAPI

Shriram K. Vasudevan, Nitin Vamsi Dantu,
Sini Raj Pulari, and T. S. Murugesh

CRC Press
Taylor & Francis Group
Boca Raton London New York

CRC Press is an imprint of the
Taylor & Francis Group, an **informa** business

First edition published 2024
by CRC Press
2385 Executive Center Drive, Suite 320, Boca Raton, FL 33431

and by CRC Press
4 Park Square, Milton Park, Abingdon, Oxon, OX14 4RN

CRC Press is an imprint of Taylor & Francis Group, LLC

© 2024 Shriram K. Vasudevan, Nitin Vamsi Dantu, Sini Raj Pulari, and T.S. Murugesh

ISBN: 9781032493107 hbk)
ISBN: 9781032493114 (pbk)
ISBN: 9781003393122 (ebk)

DOI: 10.1201/9781003393122

Typeset in Caslon
by Deanta Global Publishing Services, Chennai, India

Contents

V

Preface

oneAPI is an open, cross-architecture programming model from Intel that gives wings to the developers to use a single code base across multiple architectures to achieve accelerated computing. The oneAPI Base Toolkit contains a core set of tools and libraries for developing high-performance, data-centric applications across diverse architectures. In short, it offers a powerful performance-based programming ecosystem.

It is becoming more obvious that the future of computing is not in a single chip for everything, but in several chips for several things. The consumers can choose, combine, and match from an ocean of accelerators for their explicit requirements. The objective is to aid software developers having one set of code to be run seamlessly for all the chips.

Adapting such unified progresses, like oneAPI, offers flexibility and can get rid of the need to toil with diverse codebases, tools and programming languages. It simplifies software development and delivers relentless performance for accelerated computing without proprietary lock-in, while also assisting the integration of existing code. With oneAPI, developers can choose the best accelerator architecture for the specific problem they are trying to solve without the need to rewrite the software for the chosen architecture/platform.

Machine learning has been growing tremendously in the market and has vast application possibilities and opportunities. Learning

ML has become almost inevitable for engineers to achieve the best results and increased productivity. Many tools and software packages are available to make machine learning easier. oneAPI from Intel has been a boon to the market and many applications are being developed with it. This book explores the ML algorithms, concepts and implementation with relevant theoretical explanations and practical implementations with the latest tools which include oneAPI. The content is presented in such a way that it caters to everyone, from novice to expert level.

The installations and practices needed to get used to the Intel DevCloud, Jupyter notebook and then the machine learning workflow, which is one of the most relevant workloads nowadays, are provided. The visualization tools, the classification, regression, bagging and boosting algorithms, along with their relevant implementation codes, offers an enjoyable learning experience while also demonstrating the solid optimized performance of oneAPI. Classification problems are included to help the reader understand the power of optimization, with additional details on Intel tools provided for an enhanced development experience catering to the varying demands of readers.

GitHub links for the codes have been presented for easier accessibility.

Let's unleash the true power of our code across diverse architectures!

Authors

Dr. Shriram K. Vasudevan, Lead Technology Evangelist, Asia Pacific and Japan, Intel India Pvt. Ltd., has more than 17 years of experience in industry and academia combined. He holds a Doctorate in embedded systems. He has authored / co-authored 45 books for various publishers including Taylor & Francis, Oxford University Press, and Wiley. He also has been granted 13 patents as inventor so far. Shriram is a hackathon enthusiast and has received awards from Harvard University, AICTE, CII, Google, TDRA Dubai and many more. He has published more than 150 research articles. He was associated with L&T Technology Services before joining Intel. Dr. Vasudevan runs a YouTube channel, under his name, which has more than 38,000 subscribers and maintains a wide range of playlists on varied topics. Dr. Shriram is also a highly regarded public speaker and has participated in multiple training events. He is a oneAPI certified Instructor, ACM Distinguished Speaker, NVIDIA Certified and NASSCOM Prime Ambassador.

Mr. Nitin Vamsi Dantu, Founder and CEO, Quadran AI, Intel Innovator, USA, is a young and dynamic AI engineer with a computer science background. He is one of the youngest CEOs in the country. He is the founder and CEO of Quadron AI and is working on Deep Learning-based healthcare solutions. His focus is toward building affordable and easy-to-use healthcare solutions. He has a dozen papers published in top journals and conferences. He is also a winner of the TDRA Award from the Government of the UAE. He has received awards from P&G, CITI, AWS and many other high-ranking companies for his skillset and contributions. He is currently pursuing research at Northeastern University in the USA.

Ms. Sini Raj Pulari, Professor and Tutor, Bahrain Polytechnic, Bahrain is a tutor at Government University (Bahrain Polytechnic, Faculty of EDICT) in the Kingdom of Bahrain, with 16 years of experience in various highly regarded Indian universities and in industry, making contributions to the teaching field and carrying out activities to maintain and develop research and professional activities relevant to computer science engineering. Her research interests include areas of Natural Language Processing, Recommender systems, Information Retrieval, Deep Learning and Machine Learning, She has authored 20-plus Scopus Indexed Publications and co-authored *Deep Learning: A Comprehensive Guide* (CRC Press/Taylor & Francis Publications, 2021). Sini has developed and guided more than 40 undergraduate and postgraduate research projects. She is an active member of the board for curriculum development for various universities. Sini has delivered more than 40 invited lectures on the applications and emerging trends in a variety of upcoming technological and research advancements. She was a speaker at a workshop in "AI for ALL" and at a workshop on the topic "Understanding Deep Learning Algorithm – Convolution Neural Networks with Real-Time Applications, Using Python, Keras and TensorFlow" and participated in a MENA Hackathon group discussion on the topic "Innovating Tech-based Solutions for Challenges in the Healthcare and Energy, Environment & Sustainability Sectors," in partnership with Tamkeen and powered by Amazon Web Services (AWS) and Elijah Coaching and Consulting Services. Sini has completed various highly reputed certifications, like Apple Certified Trainer, SCJP, Oracle Certified Associate and APQMR-Quality Matters.

Dr. T S Murugesh has experience of more than 23 years in academia in the field of Analog and Digital Electronics, Automation and Control, IoT, System design, Image Processing, Artificial Intelligence,

Machine Learning, Instrumentation and Computational Bio-engineering. After a tenure of almost 19 years with the Department of Electronics and Instrumentation Engineering, Faculty of Engineering and Technology, Annamalai University, Tamil Nadu, India, he is currently working as Associate Professor in the Department of Electronics and Communication Engineering, Government College of Engineering Srirangam, Tiruchirappalli, Tamil Nadu, India. He has delivered four talks at the international-level conferences of high repute and has also delivered invited lectures at the national level in various institutions like Sastra University, Annamalai University, Manakula Vinayagar Institute of Technology, Puducherry, Government College of Engineering Srirangam, Madurai Institute of Engineering and Technology, P.A. College of Engineering and Technology, Pollachi, Viswajyothi College of Engineering and Technology Kerala, Mahatma Gandhi University, Kottayam, Kerala, National Institute of Technology, Tiruchirappalli, Saranathan College of Engineering, Tiruchirappalli. He has also delivered invited lectures in several Faculty Development Programmes organized by the Faculty Training Centre, Government College of Technology, Coimbatore, in association with Government College of Engineering Thanjavur, Government College of Engineering Salem, India, and also appeared in a national-level webinar conducted on behalf of "Unnat Bharat Abhiyan," a flagship programme of the Ministry of Education, Government of India. He has almost 40 peer-reviewed indexed papers in journals including Springer, Springer Nature, Elsevier, Wiley, Inderscience, etc. He has organized a one-week AICTE Training And Learning (ATAL) Academy-sponsored FDP, has conducted several workshops at the national level and is a reviewer for IEEE Inderscience and many other peer-reviewed journals. He has acted as a Primary Evaluator for the Government of India's Smart India Hackathon 2022 (Software & Hardware Edition) as well as Toycathon 2021 and also as a Judge in the Grand Finale for the Government of India's "Toycathon 2021," an inter-ministerial initiative organized by Ministry of Education's Innovation Cell with support from AICTE (All-India Council for Technical Education). Murugesh has evaluated ideas for "The Kavach2023" Cybersecurity Hackathon, organized by the Ministry of Home Affairs (MHA) in collaboration with the Ministry of Education's (MoE) Innovation Cell, AICTE along with Bureau of Police Research and Development (BPR&D) and Indian Cybercrime Coordination Centre (I4C) (MHA), Government of India. He is a hackathon enthusiast, and his team has won First Prize in the 2022 CloudFest Hackathon 2 presented by Google Cloud as well as in the DigitalGov Hack, the Hackathon by WSIS Forum 2023 and Digital Government Authority, Saudi Arabia, and also won Second Prize in the IFG x TA Hub Hackathon 2022. He is a certified Mentor under the "National Initiative for Technical Teachers Training" programme conducted by the All-India Council for Technical Education (AICTE), New Delhi, and the National Institute of Technical Teachers Training and Research, Chennai, and is also a Certified Microsoft Educator Academy Professional. He was also a Master Assessor for a Naan Mudhalvan Program, 2023, devised by the Government of Tamil Nadu. He is also a reviewer of B.E./B. Tech Technical Books in the Regional Language scheme of AICTE, coordinated by the Centre for Development of Tamil in Engineering and Technology, Anna University, Tamil Nadu, India. He has mentored his college teams for the Smart India Hackathon, among which one team won First Prize for the Problem Statement "Employment tracking and traceability system – Organized sector," provided by the Ministry of Labour Employment, Government of India during the Grand Final of Smart India Hackathon, 2022 (Software Edition), August 2022. He has been recognized by Huawei for academic collaboration and was issued Huawei Developers Certification. He is a Conference Committee Member as well as a Publishing Committee Member of the International Association of Applied Science and Technology. He holds editorial board membership of the *American Journal of Embedded Systems and Applications.* He was also a Technical Program Committee member for the Springer-sponsored, Scopus-Indexed International Conference on Recent Developments in Cyber Security (ReDCySec-2023) conducted by the Center for Cyber Security and Cryptology (CCSC), Sharda University, Greater Noida, Uttar Pradesh, India. He was a chairperson for a Plenary Session in the International Hybrid Conference on Nano Structured Materials and Polymers (ICNP 2023) at Mahatma Gandhi University Kerala, India during 2023. He has held various academic responsibilities such as Chairman for Anna University Central Valuation, Chief Superintendent for the Anna University Theory Examinations and is presently the Exam Cell Coordinator for his institution. He also holds the professional body membership of the Institution of Engineers (India). He has co-authored three books for CRC Press/Taylor & Francis Group (UK) and is currently co-authoring one book each for Nova Science Publishers, USA and CRC Press.

1

Intel oneAPI

An Introductory Discussion

Learning Objectives

After reading this chapter, the reader should be able to understand the following:

- Why oneAPI?
- What is there for us in oneAPI?
- Features and learning resources of oneAPI.

1.1 Introduction

What is oneAPI? Well, this is a question asked by many tech enthusiasts, learners, teachers, industry practitioners and everyone in the tech space. This chapter is intended to provide information as to what oneAPI is all about, why there is a lot of discussion about oneAPI, what oneAPI can provide, etc. (Note: It is oneAPI and not OneAPI.)

Let us first understand the problem faced by software developers all around the world.

Firstly, there has been humongous growth recently in specialized workloads. Secondly, each hardware needs to use different programming languages and related libraries. This increases the challenges with respect to maintaining different code bases and repositories. Thirdly, though it is seen as an advantage with the increase in the number of tools, it is also a challenge for developers to learn to use different tools, particularly given the learning time involved. What we mean here is that the development of software for different hardware platforms like CPU (Central Processing Unit), GPU (Graphics Processing Unit) or FPGA (Field-Programmable Gate Array) requires different learning strategies, investments and eventually no guarantee of reusing that work with other architectures/hardware. Writing code

DOI: 10.1201/9781003393122-1

1

once, then writing it again for another architecture is the biggest bug-bear faced by software developers globally. Yes, this problem has to be solved and this is where oneAPI comes in.

One can understand the aforesaid point by referring to Figure 1.1. The figure presented is self-explanatory. The challenge to be solved is huge and that is where oneAPI comes in handy.

One must first understand what oneAPI is all about. It is an open and standards-based multi-architecture programming model which addresses the programmers' challenges. oneAPI provides the developers with total freedom and choice to select the hardware as CPU, GPU, or FPGA for enhanced computing. The vision behind the oneAPI's creation is interesting. It aims to bring a unified software development environment across CPU, GPU and other accelerators.

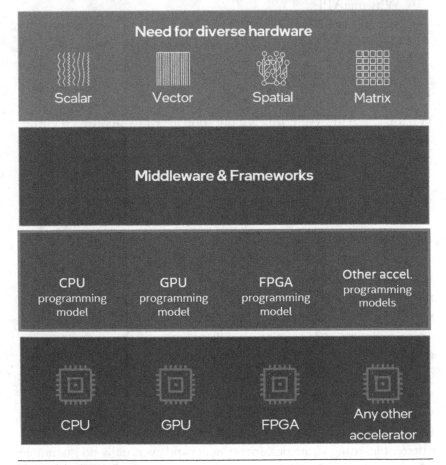

Figure 1.1   The challenge.

oneAPI is an industry initiative and is completely based on standards and open specifications.

oneAPI has many features which developers certainly appreciate:

- First and foremost, developers can develop and deploy the software with absolute peace of mind.
- oneAPI includes libraries and has a unified language that can ensure complete native code performance.
- Freedom. oneAPI facilitates the native code performance across a range of hardware including CPUs, GPUs, FPGAs and AI (Artificial Intelligence) accelerators.
- Since it is of open-industry standards, it is certainly the best approach for the future.
- The biggest advantage lies with the excellent compatibility of oneAPI with the existing programming languages, including C++, Python, SYCL, Fortran and openMP languages.

oneAPI is the foundational or base programming stack. One should see it as a facilitator to optimize the middleware and the upstream frameworks. One can achieve a clearer understanding of this point from Figure 1.2. The reader can see that TensorFlow kind of frameworks sit above oneAPI, which is optimized for performance. The representation shown in Figure 1.2 is enhanced and presented in Figure 1.3 for extra clarity.

The optimized applications go to the uppermost layer as one can see from Figure 1.3, which leverages the middleware and the frameworks.

oneAPI comes with powerful and advanced porting toolkits (this eases our job, folks, as it ports the code for us). Analysis tools, like the intel VTune profiler, intel advisor and debuggers, are also provided. This enables someone to debug the code or to analyse the performance across all levels of abstraction without any hindrance.

Having explained what oneAPI is and what it brings to you as a developer, it is important to talk about another very important benefit oneAPI offers to developers. There is no proprietary lock-in associated with oneAPI and it is compatible with the code written in native languages such as C, C++ and more, as described earlier.

In simple words, oneAPI provides developers with the option to choose the best of the architecture for a specific problem without

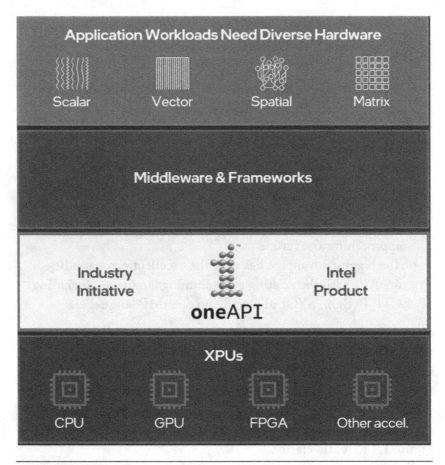

Figure 1.2 The revolution – oneAPI (the industry initiative and Intel product).

forcing the developer to re-write the code for different architectures or platforms.

oneAPI also promotes community and industry collaboration on a larger scale.

Remember this – oneAPI is all about "Write once, deploy many times!"

1.2 Approaches – Direct Programming and API-Based Programming

oneAPI is interesting. There are two options provided to developers for programming: direct programming and API-based programming. In addition, DPC++ provides the compatibility tool and the debug tools with oneAPI (see Figure 1.4).

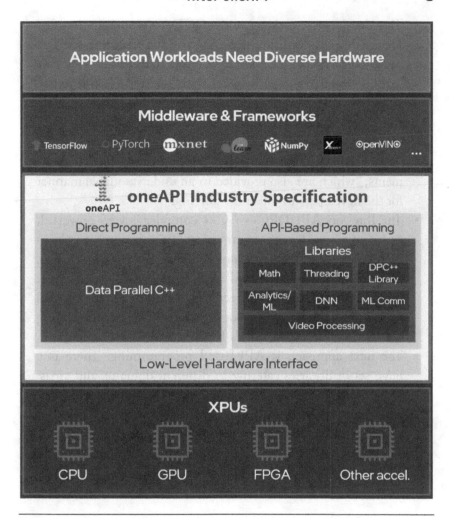

Figure 1.3 Power of oneAPI.

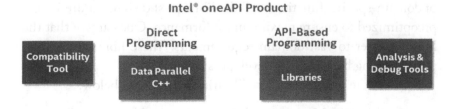

Figure 1.4 Programming model.

- The developers working with CUDA (Compute Unified Device Application) find that migrating the existing CUDA code (CUDA Source Code) to the (Data Parallel C++) DPC++ (DPC++ Source Code) is easier with oneAPI. oneAPI provides you with the Intel DPC++ Compatibility Tool to migrate source code from CUDA to DPC++ with ease. There is a lot of assistance available with the migration, with almost 80–90% being carried out automatically. The best part is "inline comments," which are also provided in an understandable manner for the developers to finish the porting.
- The Intel oneAPI DPC++ / C++ compiler is very powerful, and it supports direct programming. This approach comes in useful when the APIs are not available for the algorithms. The reader will be presented with more details about direct programming later. For direct programming, Data Parallel C++ is an evolution of C++ for productive data-centric coding that will target CPUs, GPUs FPGAs and AI accelerators.
- The next approach is API-based programming. There is a huge set of libraries catering to different domains and areas. Details of the libraries are presented in the following section, where readers will find a lot of information. Developers can just go ahead and use them without any challenge.
- Finally, in Figure 1.4, you can also see that the tools like Intel VTune Profiler and Intel Advisor are present, which can help in analyzing the performance.

1.3 Libraries – More Power to You

oneAPI comes with a rich set of libraries, which enable the acceleration of domain-specific functions. All the libraries shown in Figure 1.5 are preoptimized to ensure maximum performance. One can see that the libraries cater to vast domain requirements. These libraries simplify programming by providing developers with APIs.

A brief note on each of these libraries is presented below:

- *Intel oneAPI Math Kernel Library*: One could use this library to develop the highly optimized math routines in their applications.

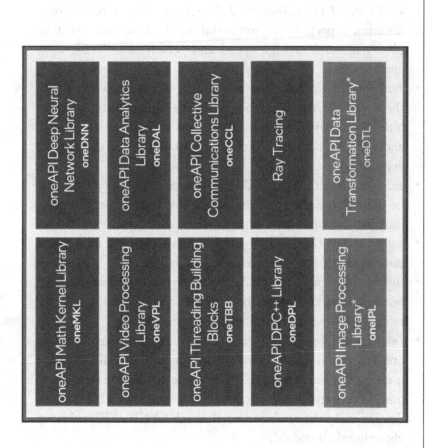

Figure 1.5 Power of oneAPI.

- *Intel oneAPI Deep Neural Network Library*: One could use this library to build the deep learning applications which use the neural networks optimized for the Intel hardware, be it processor or graphics.
- *Intel oneAPI Video Processing Library*: As the name indicates, this library can be very handy to accelerate video processing in the chosen application.
- *Intel oneAPI Data Analytics Library*: This is one of the best libraries, especially for industrial needs. One can use this library to combine high speed and performance in big data applications.
- *Intel oneAPI Threading Building Blocks*: Often known as TBB, these provide the developer with the opportunity to combine the TBB-based parallelism on the Multicore CPUs and the SYCL device-accelerated parallelism in the chosen application.
- *Intel oneAPI Collective Communications Library*: This can be used where the applications focus primarily on the deep learning and machine learning workloads.
- *Intel oneAPI DPC++ Library*: One can use this library for building high-performance parallel applications.
- *Support in the form of Ray Tracing libraries*: These libraries can be used to build photorealistic visuals, from studio animation to scientific and industrial visualizations.
- *Intel oneAPI Image Processing Library*: As the name implies, oneAPI contains image processing functionality, filters, geometric transformations, color and type conversions and various 3D operations that allow developers to take advantage of diverse computational devices through SYCL* APIs without changing their code(s).
- *Intel oneAPI Data Transformation Library (DTL)*: This is a very innovative attempt from Intel to provide ready-to-use, optimized data compression functions for diverse architectures. OneDTL is designed in such a way that execution can be carried out on a wide range of devices, including CPUs, GPUs, etc.

It is now time for the reader to understand the toolkits. Intel oneAPI has a plethora of toolkits available, offering a wide range of services. These will be explored in Chapter 2.

1.4 What's the Connection between oneAPI and This Book?

Well, this should be in the mind of the reader by now. Let's answer that question. Machine learning (ML) concepts can be taught through various platforms and modes. For this book, we have chosen oneAPI. We believe that machine learning will be easier through this approach. In addition, oneAPI is currently the need of the hour for industry. ML skills, hand in hand with oneAPI knowhow, will be phenomenal. We are certain that the reader will enjoy this entire journey of learning.

Resources

One of the greatest things Intel has done is to provide excellent learning resources for all levels of expertise. From novice to expert, the materials and learning pathways provided are simply outstanding. Intel also provides case studies, reference codes through GIT, and more for the learners. Teachers have the opportunity to become certified instructors for oneAPI and they can get access to complete training materials, presentations, example codes, assignment questions and answers.

The links below can be used to learn more about oneAPI,

- Intro to oneAPI
  https://www.intel.com/content/www/us/en/developer/tools/
  oneapi/overview.html#gs.d912h6
- oneAPI Toolkits
  https://www.intel.com/content/www/us/en/developer/tools/
  oneapi/toolkits.html#gs.3ovxmi
- Learning Paths
  https://www.intel.com/content/www/us/en/developer/tools/
  oneapi/training/overview.html
- Community Projects
  https://devmesh.intel.com/
- oneAPI DevCloud
  https://devcloud.intel.com/oneapi/

To become a certified instructor for oneAPI, one can go ahead and apply to https://www.intel.com/content/www/us/en/secure/developer /oneapi/certified-instructor-apply.html

And remember, it is all free!

1.5 Key Points to Remember

1. oneAPI is an industry initiative and is a standard-based open programming model.
2. There are two options provided to developers for programming with oneAPI. One is direct programming, and the second option is API-based programming.
3. oneAPI provides you with the Intel DPC++ Compatibility Tool to migrate source code from CUDA to DPC++ with ease.
4. oneAPI comes with tools like Intel VTune Profiler and Intel Advisor which can help in analyzing the performance.
5. oneAPI comes with a rich set of libraries which enable acceleration of domain-specific functions.
6. Readers need not get carried away with the above huge list! We shall make sure that learning is imparted in the way it should be done.

Well, we sincerely hope you enjoyed this quite detailed introductory discussion on oneAPI. It's time to move on and explore the Intel oneAPI toolkits, so let's move on to the next chapter.

Quiz Questions (Answer It Yourself, Folks!)

1. What is oneAPI?
2. What are the major benefits of oneAPI which one could cite?
3. State the names of the oneAPI libraries.
4. Code once, reuse as often as you wish – how is this possible with oneAPI?
5. How is VTune Profiler helpful for developers?
6. How can someone use the Intel advisor to gain better results?
7. Explain the programming model supported by oneAPI.

2

THE Intel oneAPI TOOLKITS

An Exploration

Learning Objectives

After going through this chapter, readers should be able to understand the following:

- What are the oneAPI toolkits?
- What are the features of the oneAPI toolkits.
- Installation guidelines.
- Resources.

2.1 Intel oneAPI Toolkits

With the 2022.3.1 release, Intel oneAPI provided a rich set of toolkits that could cater to a variety of domains and applications. With these oneAPI toolkits, one can build, analyze and even optimize performance-improved, cross-architecture applications on the CPU, GPU or any other accelerator. The toolkits also present developers with excellent libraries, optimized frameworks and excellent and easy-to-use tools for debugging.

These toolkits are designed with performance as the major target while also lowering the cost of software development and with a reduced maintenance cost. oneAPI and the toolkits certainly make developers more productive.

The following are the oneAPI toolkits made available by Intel for the developers to explore and use. (Refer Figure 2.1)

    a. *Intel oneAPI Base Toolkit*: It all starts with the oneAPI Base Toolkit which has a pack of high-performance tools for building applications with C++, DPC++ and more. Developers can build data-centric applications across diverse architectures with the help of this toolkit. You can complement the Base Kit with

DOI: 10.1201/9781003393122-2   **11**

additional toolkits. The toolkit comes with a bundle of tools and libraries, and they are listed below for quick reference:

- oneAPI Collective Communications Library.
- oneAPI Data Analytics Library.
- oneAPI Deep Neural Networks Library.
- oneAPI DPC++ Compiler.
- oneAPI DPC++ Library.
- oneAPI Math Kernel Library.
- oneAPI Threading Building Blocks.
- oneAPI Video Processing Library.
- Intel Advisor.
- Intel Distribution for Python*.
- Intel DPC++ Compatibility Tool.
- Intel FPGA Add-On for oneAPI Base Toolkit (optional).
- Intel Integrated Performance Primitives.
- Intel VTune™ Profiler.
- GDB.

The reader can refer to Figure 2.1 to understand how the Intel oneAPI Base Toolkit supports developers with direct programming, API-based programming and a rich array of libraries.

The features that the oneAPI Base Toolkit bring in are enormous and are summarized as a diagrammatic representation in Figure 2.2 for easier reference.

One can install the oneAPI Base Toolkit in the machine and develop applications or can use DevCloud to develop applications seamlessly. The latter option is easier for the developer as the need for installation or setting up the environment is not great.

The installation procedure for all the mentioned kits remains almost the same. The only variable is that the executable file to be downloaded and the corresponding links could be different.

One can download the oneAPI Base Toolkit from the link: https://www.intel.com/content/www/us/en/developer/tools/oneapi/base-toolkit-download.html.

But it is important to know if the user's system has the requirements met for the installation to be carried out. One can learn the requirements from the link: https://www.intel.com/content/www/us/en/developer/articles/system-requirements/intel-oneapi-base-toolkit-system-requirements.html.

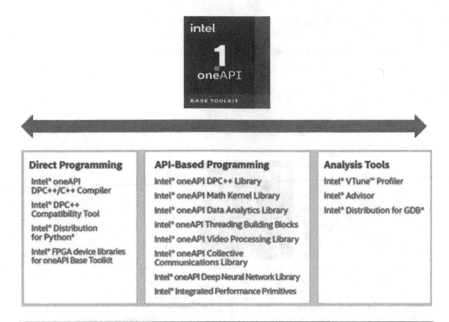

Figure 2.1 Richness of the oneAPI Base Toolkit.

The oneAPI Base Toolkit is available for MacOS, Windows and Linux (Figure 2.3). Based on what the user's operating system is, the download can be initiated.

One can prefer online, or offline distribution as required. Below is the screenshot (Figure 2.4) presenting the options (online or offline options are available for all the supported operating systems).

If the online mode of installation is selected, one would get the executable file downloaded immediately and it is lightweight one (13 MB). If the offline option is selected, the executable file is heavy (6 GB) and may need a little more time to complete the download process. Both the options are fine, and the users can choose according to their requirements. There may be a signup request for the download to be accomplished. One can see the volume of the installation file for offline and online modes presented in Figure 2.5.

The user is presented with a walk-through of the offline installation procedure. The operations and sequences remain the same with the online mode of installation as well.

The first step is to specify the path for the extraction of the product package. Figure 2.6 indicates the path to be specified.

It takes a few seconds for the extraction to be completed (Figure 2.7).

Efficient Integration with the legacy
code. The DPC++ compatibility tool
helps in easier migration, efficiently as
well.

intel.

1

oneAPI

BASE TOOLKIT

Freedom of choice (Don't rewrite
software for different hardware,
instead innovate)

Fast and Efficient – Rich libraries and
Advanced Tools

Get the fullest advantage of the
performance across the Architectures,
Accelerate performance across the
Intel CPU, GPU or Other accelerators

Figure 2.2   The features of the oneAPI Base Toolkit.

Get the Intel® oneAPI Base Toolkit
No Transistor Left Behind™
The Smart Path to Accelerated Computing without the Economic and Technical Burdens of Proprietary Programming Models

Select options below to download

Select operating system
Windows
macOS
Linux

Figure 2.3   Operating system support.

Select options below to download

Windows   ^   Select distribution   ⌄
                                               Online
                                               Offline

Figure 2.4   Installation options.

Figure 2.5   Installation options.

The next step in the sequence is interesting. The installer will automatically check the system requirements. One can refer to Figure 2.8 to understand this. On clicking "Continue" in the pop-up shown below, the system requirement checks begin automatically.

The complete details of what is getting installed with the oneAPI Base Toolkit are shown once the system check is completed. Also, one must agree to the license agreement. The user can also customise the installation, if required (Figure 2.9). On clicking "Continue," the installation will progress further. It may take some time for the entire process to be completed.

To make life easier, the installer will prompt if the integration with the Integrated Development Environment (IDE) needs to be carried out; the options presented are as shown in Figure 2.10. Though this is an optional step, it is preferred to be integrated with the IDE (Microsoft Visual Studio 2022).

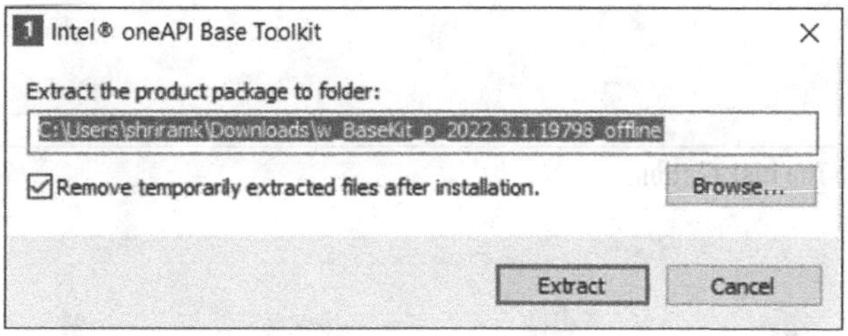

Figure 2.6   Extraction path.

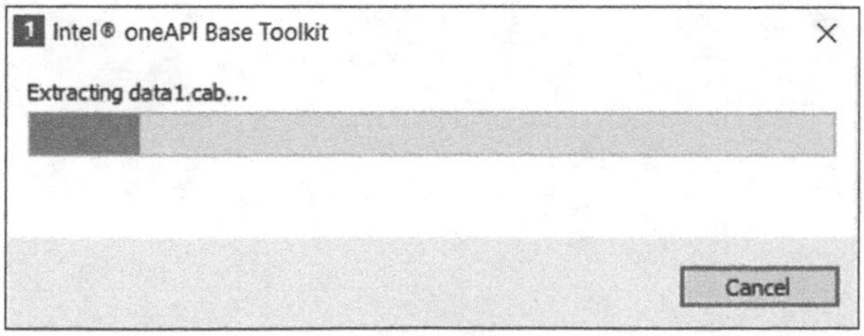

Figure 2.7   Extraction progress.

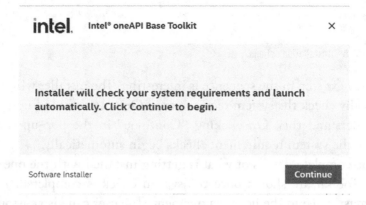

Figure 2.8 System requirements check.

Figure 2.9 The installation.

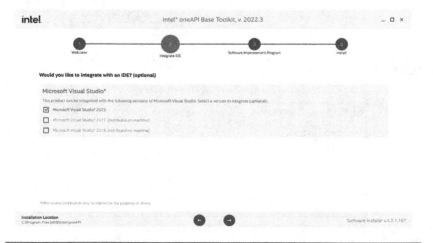

Figure 2.10 IDE integration.

Subsequently, the intel software improvement program will now appear, and the user is free to give consent for data collection, or otherwise (Figure 2.11).

That is it! The installation will begin (Figure 2.12). The user can sit back and relax for a while.

When the installation is completed (Figure 2.13), and there is no stoppage, one can go ahead and innovate as required with the Intel oneAPI Base Toolkit.

The options for building and running the projects with the visual studio command line are also available and can be referred to at the

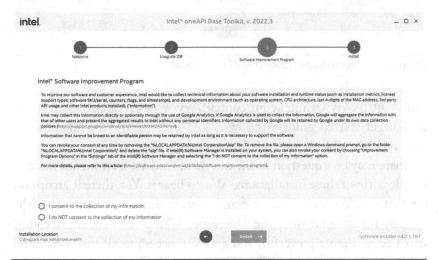

Figure 2.11   Software improvement program – consent for data collection.

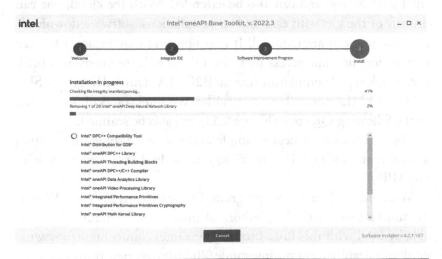

Figure 2.12   Seamless installation of oneAPI Base Toolkit.

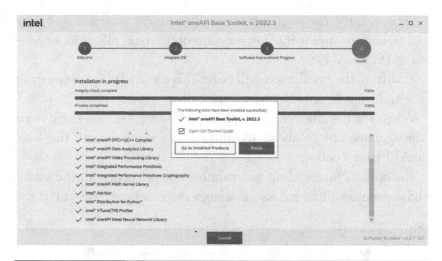

Figure 2.13   Successful installation of oneAPI Base Toolkit.

link: https://www.intel.com/content/www/us/en/docs/oneapi-base-toolkit/get-started-guide-windows/2023-0/run-project-visual-studio-command-line.html

There may be a question in the minds of readers! Can we not make it simple without these installations? We do hear it. Yes, there is an option for that too. You can build, test and even optimize your project without any investment using the Developer Cloud (DevCloud) account. It is free and more powerful, and gets you access to all the latest Intel hardware, including the CPUs, GPUs or FPGAs. Access is given by Intel for 120 days and can also be extended. With the cloud, one can use any of the kits with ease and no installations, software downloads or configurations are required. It is simple and easy to use. One can register for the same access with the this link: https://consumer.intel.com/intelcorpb2c.onmicrosoft.com/B2C_1A_UnifiedLogin_SISU_CML_SAML/generic/login?entityId=www.intel.com&ui_locales=en or the following QR code (Figure 2.14) can also be scanned.

The registration process is simple and may need some information as your name and email id. That's it, you can build your solutions with oneAPI!

What next? Gear up and program. One can learn the oneAPI programming easily with the plethora of information being made available by intel with this link: https://www.intel.com/content/www/us/en/docs/oneapi/programming-guide/2023-0/overview.html

Figure 2.14 Intel DevCloud registration link.

b. *Intel oneAPI HPC (high-performance computing) Toolkit*: The name says it all. This toolkit, as one can understand, is domain specific. With this toolkit, one can build and deliver fast Fortran, OpenMP and MPI applications that combine high-performance computing applications with cutting-edge techniques.

    The toolkit comes with a bundle of tools and libraries, and they are listed below for the reader's quick reference:

- C++ Compiler
- Cluster Checker
- Fortran Compiler
- Intel Inspector
- Intel MPI Library
- Intel Trace Analyzer and Collector

    The installation procedure remains almost the same as was discussed for the Intel oneAPI Base Toolkit section. However, the installable is to be downloaded from the link: https://www.intel.com/content/www/us/en/developer/tools/oneapi/hpc-toolkit-download.html. The rest of the guidelines remain the same. Some of the toolkits may demand the installation of the Base Toolkit as a prerequisite, which will be clearly indicated by the checker at the beginning of the installation.

c. *Intel oneAPI Internet of Things (IoT) Toolkit*: This is also a domain-specific toolkit. With this IoT toolkit one, could accelerate the development of smart and connected devices leading to endless innovations. This toolkit is bundled with:

- Intel Inspector
- Intel oneAPI DPC++/C++ Compiler
- Intel® C++ Compiler Classic

The installation procedure is almost the same as discussed earlier for the Intel oneAPI Base Toolkit. However, the installable is to be downloaded from the link https://www.intel.com/content/www/us/en/developer/tools/oneapi/iot-toolkit-download.html.

d. *Intel oneAPI Rendering Kit*: This kit is for the creative folks. Yes, the guys working on the visualization and related areas can use this kit to create performant, high-fidelity visualization applications. The toolkit is very interesting for developers to use and develop stunning results, and it contains a handful of tools as listed below:

- Embree
- Implicit SPMD Program Compiler
- Open Volume Kernel Library
- Open Image Denoise
- OpenSWR
- OSPRay
- OSPRay Studio
- OSPRay for Hydra
- Rendering Toolkit Utilities

The installation procedure will take almost as long as that for the Intel oneAPI Base Toolkit. However, the installable is to be downloaded from the link: https://www.intel.com/content/www/us/en/developer/tools/oneapi/rendering-toolkit-download.html.

e. *Intel AI Analytics Toolkit*: This is one of the best toolkits, and industry is already heaping accolades onto this toolkit. With this toolkit in place, one could accelerate machine learning and data science pipelines with optimized DL (Deep Learning) frameworks and high-performing Python libraries. This toolkit is very powerful and full of resources. The toolkit comes with the following tools:

- Intel Optimization for TensorFlow
- Intel Optimization for PyTorch
- Intel Distribution for Python*
- Intel Distribution of Modin (available through Anaconda only)

- Model Zoo for Intel Architecture
- Intel Low-Precision Optimization Tool

   One can download the AI Analytics Toolkit at the link: https://www.intel.com/content/www/us/en/developer/tools/oneapi/ai-analytics-toolkit-download.html?operatingsystem=linux&distributions=zypperpackagemanager.

f. *Intel OpenVINO*: This is one of the finest toolkits. It is Open Visual Inferencing and Neural Network Optimization. One can develop and deploy high-performance inference and applications from edge to cloud with OpenVINO. OpenVINO can be downloaded and installed seamlessly with the guidelines and installable provided at https://www.intel.com/content/www/us/en/developer/tools/openvino-toolkit/overview.html.

The greatest advantage of all these toolkits is that they are free to use and easy to learn. The toolkits can be installed for Windows, Linux, or Mac OS. Also, if the developer wishes to use the DevCloud, it is also possible and requires no installation or any additional downloads. It is easy to develop and results are available instantaneously.

The next appreciable advantage is that there are so many tutorials and learning materials made available for beginners. Many case studies are presented to ensure progressive learning as well.

Well, we honestly hope the readers will have enjoyed exploring these toolkits. Let's move on to the next chapter to learn more details about the DevCloud, along with its features, power, etc.

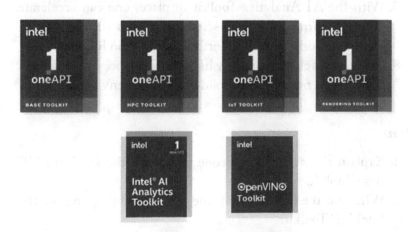

Figure 2.15   The oneAPI toolkits (some are powered by oneAPI).

Resources

- https://www.intel.com/content/www/us/en/developer/tools/oneapi/overview.html#gs.3otusu
- https://www.intel.com/content/www/us/en/developer/tools/oneapi/toolkits.html#gs.kfp7z3
- https://youtu.be/FdntPy1cCKo
- https://youtu.be/_y4bPjj8Gv4

2.2 Key Points to Remember

1. Each oneAPI toolkit comes with a bundle of tools.
2. The oneAPI toolkits can be installed directly onto the machine with the guidelines provided or one can develop applications with the DevCloud.
3. The DevCloud enables developers to develop applications with ease without any installations or configurations.
4. The oneAPI Base Toolkit has a pack of high-performance tools for building applications with C++, DPC++.
5. With the oneAPI HPC Toolkit, one can build and deliver fast Fortran, OpenMP and MPI applications that combine high-performance computing applications with cutting-edge techniques.
6. Visualization and related areas can use the oneAPI Rendering Toolkit to create performant, high-fidelity visualization applications.
7. With the AI Analytics Toolkit in place, one can accelerate machine learning and data science pipelines with optimized DL frameworks and high-performing Python libraries.
8. One can develop and deploy high-performance inference and applications from edge to cloud with the OpenVINO Toolkit.

Quiz

1. Explain the need for someone to opt for the Intel oneAPI Base Toolkit.
2. What are the features that one could get by opting for the Intel IoT Toolkit?

3. Mention the names of the libraries/packages that come with the Intel oneAPI AI analytics toolkit.
4. Which toolkit would be handy for developers working on visualization applications?
5. If someone is working on HPC applications, which toolkit would be most helpful for them?

3

THE Intel DevCloud AND JUPYTER NOTEBOOKS

Learning Objectives

After reading this chapter, the readers should be able to understand the following:

- Power of DevCloud
- Registration process
- Jupyter Notebook and DevCloud
- DevCloud Commands

3.1 Introduction

This chapter will provide a lot of insights into the fundamentals of Intel DevCloud. Also, the Jupyter Notebook is integrated with DevCloud, making learning and usage much easier for software developers. It is expected that readers should create an Intel DevCloud account to try out all the points which are being discussed in this chapter.

3.2 What Is Intel DevCloud?

The DevCloud is an interesting and powerful sandbox which enables someone to develop, test and run the workloads across a range of accelerators which include Intel CPUs, GPUs, and FPGAs with the Intel oneAPI software stack.

It comes with so many features and is power packed. Figure 3.1 presents the features of the Intel DevCloud. Coding with the DevCloud is easy, without the need to worry about hardware acquisition; more importantly, no installations or configurations are required. It also possesses excellent and easy-to-understand tutorials for developers. Above all, the support for the Jupyter Notebooks and Visual Studio code makes it stand taller than the most sought-after cloud platforms.

24

DOI: 10.1201/9781003393122-3

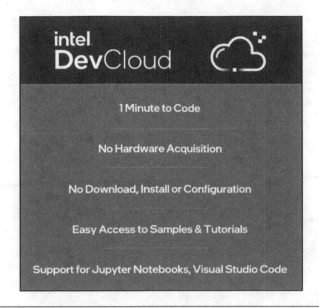

Figure 3.1   Intel DevCloud features summarized.

One can find a lot of useful information on the Intel DevCloud from the website software.intel.com/devcloud/oneapi

3.2.1 How to Create a DevCloud Account?

One can follow the step-by-step process presented below to create the DevCloud account/access created.

1. Visit the software.intel.com/devcloud/oneapi website.
    It will prompt you to fill in certain basic information which should not consume a lot of time. The screenshot presented below in Figure 3.2 reveals the information sought.
2. On completion of the above information, two more questions will be presented to you, inviting your response as presented in Figure 3.3. One can choose the appropriate answers.
    Once this is done, that's it.
3. The terms and conditions then need to be agreed. One can read the terms and conditions and agree to the same by clicking the check box. Once done, the submit button is clicked and the account is completed (Figure 3.4).
4. On filling in the details, one receives the following message (Figure 3.5) which ensures successful sign-in.

Create an Intel® DevCloud Account

Sign up for immediate access to the latest Intel technology without downloads or hardware setup.

Intel Employee? Create account here

All fields are required except any fields specifically marked as optional.

Basic Contact Information

| First Name | Last Name |

| Email Address | Username |

| Password | Confirm Password |

| Country/Region | ⌄ |

Figure 3.2   DevCloud registration – step 1.

What is your purpose for using Intel® Devcloud (Select all that apply)

☐ HPC Workloads

☐ AI Training

☐ AI Inference

| Business or Institution Name |

| What type of user are you? | ⌄ |

Communication Subscriptions
Subscribe to optional email updates from Intel

☐ Select all subscriptions below

☐ Developer Zone Newsletter

☐ Edge Software Hub Product Communication

☐ Programmable Logic Product Announcements

☐ Programmable Logic Newsletters

Figure 3.3   DevCloud registration – step 2.

5. An e-mail will be sent by DevCloud for validation and the user will be prompted to verify the email (see Figure 3.6)
6. On clicking the e-mail verification link, the process is completed. One will see the below message on the screen following the completion of the aforesaid process (Figure 3.7).

Terms and Conditions

 I have read and accept the Intel® DevCloud Agreement

By submitting this form, you are confirming you are an adult 18 years or older and you agree to share your personal information with Intel to stay connected to the latest Intel technologies and industry trends by email and telephone. You can unsubscribe at any time. Intel's web sites and communications are subject to our Privacy Notice and Terms of Use.

This site is protected by reCAPTCHA and the Google Privacy Policy and Terms of Service apply.

Submit

Figure 3.4   DevCloud registration – step 3.

Almost there!

Check your email for the verification link and **sign in.** The link will expire in 5 days.

Didn't receive the email? Check your spam or junk folder or click on Resend email below.
Click Here

Figure 3.5   DevCloud registration – step 4.

Almost Done...Please Verify Your Email

Welcome Shriram KV,

Thank you for registering for an Intel® DevCloud Account.

Please verify your email address by clicking the link below. The link will expire in 5 days.

Verify your email

Your password should be protected as confidential. Your use of the password and Intel's websites are governed by Intel's Terms and Conditions of Use linked from the bottom of each respective site's web pages.

If you have any questions, please contact us.

To manage your profile, including available marketing subscriptions, please visit My Intel.

Please DO NOT reply to this e-mail message. This is an automated response.
To ensure that you continue receiving our e-mails, please add us to your address book.

Figure 3.6   DevCloud registration – step 5.

< Sign In

Verify Your Email Address

Thank you for verifying your email address. You will be redirected to the site in a few seconds.

Sign In FAQ

Figure 3.7   DevCloud registration – step 6.

3.3 Well, It's All Done. What Next? Simple, Let's Login!

How can someone access DevCloud through "Connect with Jupyter Lab"?

Click the link https://devcloud.intel.com/oneapi/get_started/. In the bottom portion of the page, there is an option for "Connect with Jupyter Lab" (Figure 3.8)

Once the Launch Jupyter lab is clicked, it is loaded and the screen will appear for the user (Figure 3.9). The world of Jupyter Lab with DevCloud is now open.

Figure 3.8   Connect with Jupyter Lab.

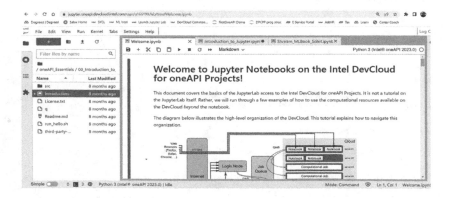

Figure 3.9   Jupyter Lab.

The new launcher button will release a plethora of options for the user. The launcher button, shown on the LHS (Left Hand Side), provides options for developers. Developers can create Python Notebooks with ease, and other options are also available. The consoles can even be chosen based on your requirements. Terminal options are also presented (Figure 3.10).

On clicking the Python 3 Notebook Launcher, the user gets the Jupyter Notebook launched with the oneAPI Kernel as shown in Figure 3.11.

Let's understand how to use the Jupyter lab, step by step.

The first step is to get the Notebook saved. From the file menu, click "Save" as an option to save the Notebook, with a desired name for the file. One can have a look at Figure 3.12 to understand same.

Jupyter Notebooks provide a great workspace, with in-browser coding, where we can define variables, work with them at our own pace, and analyse them as we go.

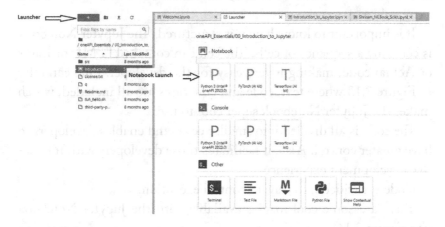

Figure 3.10   Launch Pad.

Figure 3.11   Jupyter Notebook Launch.

Figure 3.12   Save the Notebook.

Why is it named Jupyter? Jupyter is an anagram of: Julia, Python and R. Yes, you can use all of these with Jupyter.

One can write code, add beautiful markdown text, images and insert YouTube videos with ease. This makes it more versatile and extremely easy to use.

It is important to know how it is structured. The Jupyter Notebook is certainly a sequence of cells. The cell can contain HTML or Latex or Actual code, making it very easy for the developer. One can refer to Figure 3.13 where text, code and equations are all included, which makes the Jupyter Notebook super cool to use.

The code is all divided into smaller cells, and enables developers to have greater control. Also, it facilitates those developers with interactive development experience.

Code is divided into cells to control execution.

There are some cool magics available with the Jupyter Notebook (see Figure 3.14).

- *%matplotlib inline*: Display plots inline in the Jupyter Notebook
- *%%timeit*: Time how long a cell takes to execute and the same is presented below as an instance.

One can execute code from another Notebook or Python file with ease in the Jupyter Lab. Here is the option. %run filename.ipynb, where filename.ipynb is the one to be pulled for execution. One can refer to Figure 3.15 (below) to understand how to perform this task.

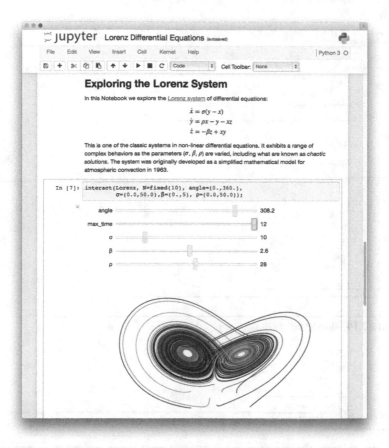

Figure 3.13   The super-flexible Jupyter Notebook.

Similarly, %load filename.py: copies the contents of the file and pastes them into the cell prescribed and the reader can try this out.

3.4 Jupyter Installation

If developers wish to install Jupyter locally in their machine and try out developments, this is also possible and this subsection summarizes it.

1. For the installation of the Jupyter, one should open the Anaconda Prompt. Many beginners will make a minor mistake here. Beginners tend to issue the command in the normal command prompt, instead of the Anaconda Prompt. This will not work as it is the destined method. The screenshot

```
import numpy as np
import matplotlib.pyplot as plt
%matplotlib inline
```

```
%%timeit
x = np.arange(10)
y = x+2
plt.plot (x ** y)
```

`336 µs ± 4.21 µs per loop (mean ± std. dev. of 7 runs, 1,000 loops each)`

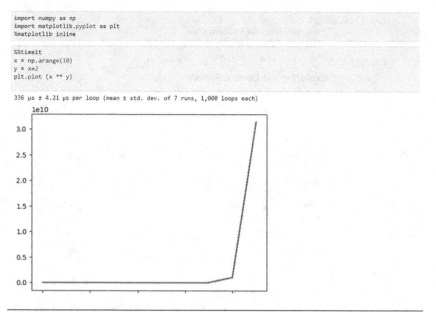

Figure 3.14   Jupyter cell magics.

Figure 3.15   The execution of another Notebook from the current one.

below presents the error message one would get if the command is issued in normal command prompt, which should be avoided. Figure 3.16 presents the command prompt followed by the error message being presented as Figure 3.17, when the command for Jupyter installation is issued.

The command to be issued is "jupyter notebook –ip=*".

2. One should open the Anaconda Prompt now and issue the above command. The following screenshots presented in Figure 3.18 reveal the presence of the Anaconda Prompt in the system. Figure 3.19 presents you with the successful Installation Note.

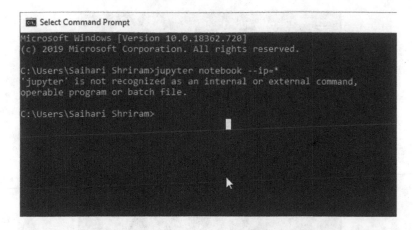

Figure 3.16   The normal Command Prompt.

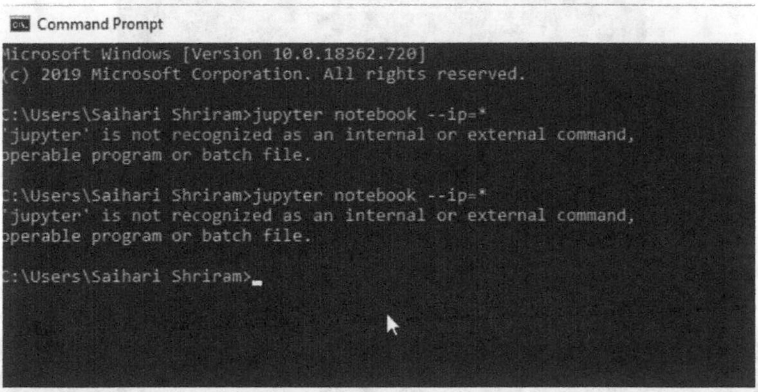

Figure 3.17   The error.

3. Once the installation is complete, one can open and access the Notebook with ease using the link obtained on successful installation. Copy and pasting the link in any of your favorite browsers will open the Jupyter Notebook.

There is another easier way to open and access the Jupyter Notebook. Just type "Jupyter" in the search box. It will display the Jupyter Notebook Launcher Option as presented below in Figure 3.21. On clicking it, the Notebook is launched.

The reader will have the Jupyter Notebook launched in a web browser as shown below in Figure 3.22.

Well, the installation is now complete, and it is time to try out the first program.

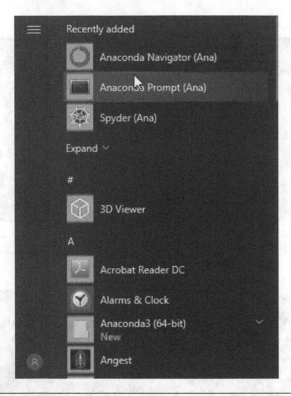

Figure 3.18   The Anaconda Prompt.

Figure 3.19   Anaconda Prompt Installation complete.

3.4.1 *The First Program with Jupyter*

1. After launching the Jupyter Notebook successfully, users are presented with the screen displayed below (Figure 3.23), where the button "New" is highlighted (Figure 3.23)
2. Once "New" is clicked, the screen below will appear, presenting the options. Click Python 3. It is a good practice to issue a

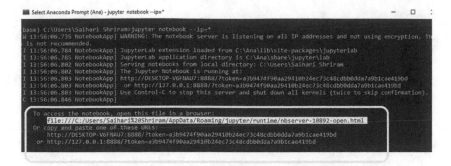

Figure 3.20   How to open Jupyter.

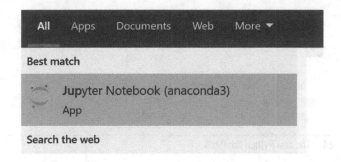

Figure 3.21   Launching Jupyter.

Figure 3.22   Jupyter – the first launch.

name for the Python Notebook which you want to create and run. The same is presented in Figure 3.24.

3. Then, the user is free to type any Python code as required. The option for running (executing) the typed code is also available and RUN has to be clicked as presented below in Figure 3.25. The output for the first code has come.

Figure 3.23   Jupyter – the first program.

Figure 3.24   The new Python Notebook.

Figure 3.25   The first code execution.

Once tested, it is always important to logout. The logout option is also highlighted and the user can click that to sign off.

The complete procedure is presented as a demo video @ https://youtu.be/bzaO9SFHJSA.

3.5 What Does DevCloud Offer Software Developers?

A developer should be elated on seeing what DevCloud can offer.

First, one can test Performance on CPU, GPU and FPGA Architectures. One can run their workloads with a range of options of accelerator options (Figure 3.26).

In addition to the above, being a developer you are provided with the following:

- Free access to Intel® oneAPI Toolkits and components and the latest Intel® hardware
- 220 GB of file storage
- 192 GB RAM
- 120 days of access (extensions available)
- Terminal Interface (Linux*)
- Microsoft Visual Studio* Code integration
- Remote Desktop for Intel® oneAPI Rendering Toolkit

Overall, one can certainly achieve the best of high-quality results with these offerings.

CPU:

- Intel® Xeon® Scalable 6128 processors
- Intel® Xeon® Scalable 8256 processors
- Intel® Xeon® E-2176 P630 processors (with Intel® Graphics Technology)

GPU:

- Intel® Xeon® E-2176 P630 processors (with Intel® Graphics Technology)
- Intel® Iris® Xe MAX

FPGA:

- Intel® Arria® 10 FPGAs
- Intel® Stratix® 10 FPGAs

Figure 3.26   The Accelerator Options.

3.6 DevCloud Terminal Commands

One can open launch the terminal by clicking the + button, which will lead to opening the terminal. This can be seen in Figure 3.27.

On successful launch, one could access the terminal and run all the traditional Linux/Unix commands with ease (see Figure 3.28 to visualize the same). For beginners or someone who needs recap of the Linux commands, it is good to visit https://devcloud.intel.com/oneapi /documentation/shell-commands/

Well, we hope the reader will have enjoyed this chapter on Intel DevCloud and the Jupyter Notebook. Let's focus our attention now toward Machine Learning, which awaits you in Chapter 4.

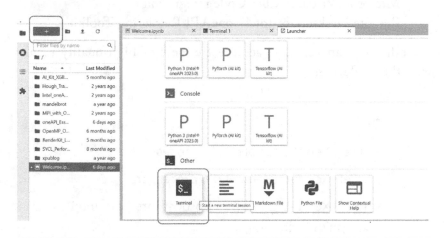

Figure 3.27   Launch the terminal.

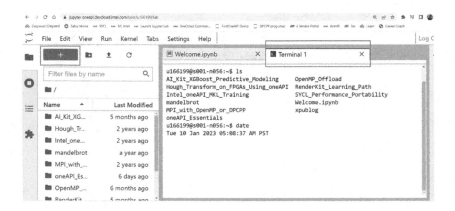

Figure 3.28   The Shell Commands.

Resources

1. https://jupyter.org/
2. https://www.intel.com/content/www/us/en/developer/tools/
   devcloud/overview.html
3. https://devcloud.intel.com/oneapi/documentation/shell
   -commands/
4. https://devcloud.intel.com/oneapi/

Exercises

Note: This chapter is mostly concerned with the installations and practice necessary for the reader to get used to Intel DevCloud, Jupyter Notebook, etc. Hence, there are no quiz questions. Instead, exercise questions are presented for the readers to try out and obtain hands-on experience.

1. Create an Intel DevCloud Account.
2. Try logging into the Intel DevCloud and open the Jupyter Notebook.
3. Try out simple Python programs with the Jupyter Notebook and oneAPI Kernel.
4. Launch a terminal and try out the shell commands.

4
WHAT IS MACHINE LEARNING?

An Introduction!

Learning Objectives

After reading this chapter, the reader should be able to understand the following:

- What is machine learning?
- Relationship between artificial intelligence (AI), machine learning (ML) and deep learning DL).
- Types of machine learning.
- Need for machine learning.
- The machine learning framework.
- Machine learning *vs* deep learning.
- Machine learning applications.

4.1 Introduction

The term machine learning (ML), belonging to the research field of Artificial Intelligence (AI), has been buzzing around us for quite a few decades. Most of us have already carried out some attempts to understand "what the word level abstract meaning is," at least by performing a Google search. Even if you have not done that, don't worry: you are in the right place to learn in-depth about "What is machine learning?" from a technical perspective. The intention of this chapter doesn't stop there – we will dive a little deeper to understand the various types of machine learning, its application to real-life scenarios and the differences between ML and Deep Learning (DL).

DOI: 10.1201/9781003393122-4

4.2 What Is Machine Learning?

Okay, let's start by taking you back to your memorable childhood. Do you ever remember how many times you fell before you started walking properly? Oh, that's a pretty old memory for you to recollect, probably we should direct this question to your parents. Let's consider an example that you might remember even now. Every one of us had a favorite kindergarten teacher, who was so sweet and patient to us. Yes, I used the word "patient" intentionally. You know why! I still remember the way my KG teacher taught me what an apple was. She literally brought the real apple and handed it over to me, asked me to play with it to experience and tell me that was an apple. In fact, she did this for almost a week.

Next week, she brought a tomato and an apple and asked me to tell her which one was the apple. I was able to correctly point out the apple without any hesitation.

Now let's come to the point: what do you think the teacher did to make the student recognize it so well! Yes, the teacher patiently

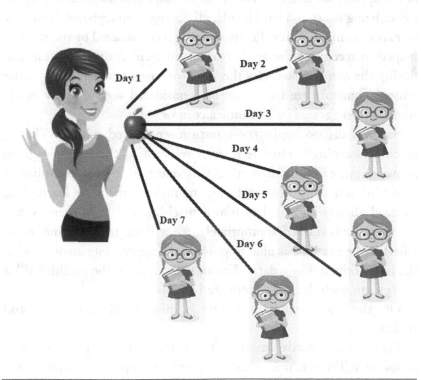

Figure 4.1   Teacher showing (training) the student for a week "what is an apple?"

Figure 4.2   Teacher testing the student if they correctly recognize the apple.

trained the student with an original apple for a week and the features of the apple, such as its red color, round shape and its internal properties of being white and hard inside, all having been registered properly by experiencing it. This collective intelligence gathered by the student helped to recognize the apple from a different fruit, like a tomato, during the *testing* phase. (By the way, we haven't conveyed anything wrong! Tomatoes are fruits that are considered vegetables by nutritionists, as suggested by Britannica.com ☺.)

So, let's discuss again the question we started with: "What is machine learning?" How is it even relevant to the example given above? Now, carefully answering this question, by the meaning of "machine learning," we are trying to make a machine learn. Yes, we feed already-known data into a machine and *train* them. Once the machine is trained appropriately, we will *test* the machine to see whether the machine is able to provide the appropriate answers with the help of the training data. We can keep training the machine till it provides us with the most optimized results.

Oh, that's all, isn't it? Machine learning is all simple now and makes sense.

Figure 4.3 correctly describes the machine learning process in a simple way. The machine takes a picture of an apple as an input, manually extracts the features of the apple and uses the information to

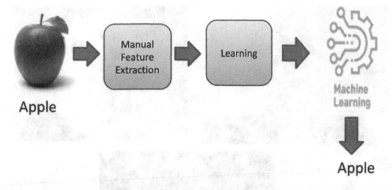

Figure 4.3 Machine learning process.

learn. This is basically done by various machine learning algorithms which are available to create a ML-trained model. This ML-trained model is provided with test data to check whether the model identifies the apple accurately or not. The major point to be noted here is that, in any machine learning process, feature extraction is very important and could be done without human intervention.

4.3 Relationship between AI, ML and DL

Artificial Intelligence (AI) is the broad area of research where researchers started thinking of introducing intelligence into machines. You may all know Sophia, the first humanoid robot who has citizenship of Saudi Arabia. Tang Yu is the AI-driven virtual robot CEO, who has been appointed to optimize operational efficiency. The whole concept of AI in the metaverse swirls around the fact that people don't need to face any real-life risks as they do in a real-life environment.

In this epoch of AI, ML is a beautiful subset of AI, which allows one to perform a specific task without any explicit interventions. Data from the past is provided to the system, the system extract features and learns from the patterns identified. Certain inferences are made from patterns and, accordingly, intelligent decisions are taken. Machine learning algorithms are auto-adaptive and hence no explicit human interventions are required for the learning process of models. Feature extraction is an important step in the whole process which helps the model to predict or classify the data appropriately.

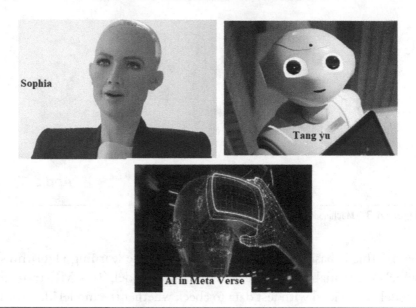

Figure 4.4   Humanoid robot Sophia, Robert CEO Tang Yu and AI in Metaverse.

Deep learning (DL) is an advanced subset of AI, where a human brain is imitated in the processing and understanding of data. Neural networks tend to be the basis of deep learning, which mainly acts like a black box to grab data and yield wonderful insights. Interpreting the results from the deep neural networks requires good analytical skills so that the output obtained makes sense for other useful applications.

Figure 4.5 shows the relationship between AI, ML and DL. Some of the major applications of AI include natural language processing (NLP), visual perception by visualization techniques, automated programming platforms like no code, AI-driven robots for strenuous jobs and household jobs, knowledge representation and reasoning.

Machine learning uses many algorithms like regression, classification, principal component analysis, clustering, etc. to detect the inferences from the data analyzed, using the models created. Multilayer perceptrons used in neural networks, with the help of various algorithms like CNN (convolutional neural networks), RNN (recurrent neural networks), GAN (generative adversarial networks), automatic feature extraction and prediction or classification, could be achieved using deep learning. The evolution of various categories of algorithm is portrayed in Figure 4.6.

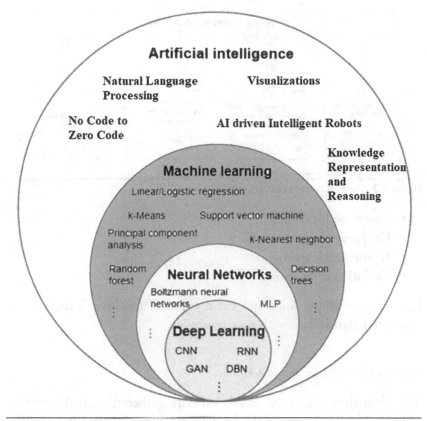

Figure 4.5 Relationship between AI, ML and DL.

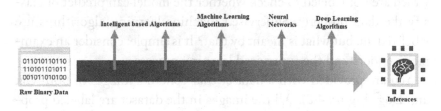

Figure 4.6 Evolutionary progress of various algorithms.

4.4 Types of Machine Learning

Now that we have a deep understanding of the place of machine learning in the AI field of research, it is time for us to understand the various types of machine learning algorithms. Machine learning algorithms are mainly classified into three categories, as given below, although we can add a fourth category for in-depth understanding (see Figure 4.7).

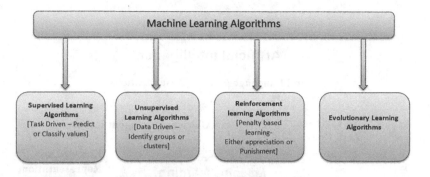

Figure 4.7   Types of machine Learning algorithms.

- Supervised learning.
- Unsupervised learning.
- Reinforced learning.
- Evolutionary learning.

Let's have a deeper look into these types of machine learning and associated algorithms, with easy examples.

4.4.1 Supervised Learning Algorithms

This algorithm makes use of labeled data gathered from the past to train the model and make the model predict or classify the test data, which are not labeled to check whether the model can predict or classify the data properly. Supervised machine learning algorithms use labeled data, but what is meant by that? It is simple: consider an example to understand the supervised learning process.

You are provided with a dataset that contains images of both Cat and Dog (Figure 4.8). All the images in the dataset are labeled properly; let's say you have 1000 images of each of Cat and Dog. You are creating a supervised learning model where you train the model using 700 labeled Cat data and 700 labeled Dog data. You have kept 300 Cat and 300 Dog images as test data (Figure 4.9). Once the supervised machine learning model is created, we will make the model predict these test data and check the accuracy of the model created.

As we now understand what's in the datasets, we shall proceed with the process.

The complete supervised learning process is described in Figure 4.10. In the supervised learning model, we work with labeled

Figure 4.8 Sample – cat- and dog-labeled training dataset.

cat_or_dog_1.jpg   cat_or_dog_2.jpg

Figure 4.9 Sample test dataset with names as cat_or _dog_1 and cat_or _dog_2.

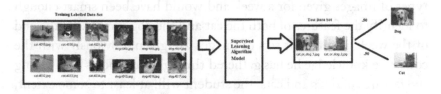

Figure 4.10 The complete supervised learning process.

data, which are fed into the model for training; once the model is trained, test data are fed into the model to either classify or predict the test data. The accuracy of model prediction is usually calculated as an evaluation metric to understand the efficacy of the trained model.

One major point to be noted here is that, if the model is trained using wrong labeled data, of course, the model will predict in a wrong manner. Hence, the training data fed to the model need to be appropriately labeled ones. Another scenario might be where the model is trained with a certain labeled dataset but an entirely new dataset is given for prediction; the percentage accuracy will be extremely low. This is quite understandable. If you have Cats and Dogs in the dataset, which is given for training the model, and if you give the test dataset as Crocodile images, there is a higher chance that the trained model might not be able to predict or will incorrectly predict the data.

Figure 4.1, depicting a teacher teaching a student about the apple, is also an example of supervised learning. Maybe you should revisit that example once again to register the concept well in your mind.

4.4.2 Unsupervised Learning Algorithm

This approach is different from the supervised learning model, as there are no labels associated with the data. Also, there is no explicit training and testing phases in the unsupervised learning method. Oh, is this not confusing? Then, how will the model be able to predict? Yes, there is a way, and we can understand it by using the following simple example.

Consider that a student is given a dataset with a set of dog and cat images, with absolutely no labels (Figure 4.11). Everyday, this dataset is given to the student and, after a week, the student is asked to group together the similar images in the dataset. What do you think the student will do? The student has been going through the different types of images given for a week and would have been smart enough to identify the features of both the cat and the dog images. By the end of the week, if different sets of images are given, obviously with the collective knowledge he has gathered through the process of mapping the features of dogs and cats, the student will, at least to some extent, map or group the cat and dog images properly. Yes, there are some cutie dogs that resemble cats, but we can't help that – hence, there may be some misclassifications.

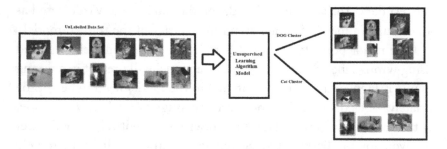

Figure 4.11   The unsupervised learning process.

Given a set of data, the algorithm will categorize them and give this categorization as the output. Each category (dog, cat) is referred to as a cluster. The labels for the clusters are to be manually tagged later. The categorization is based on the features in the data points. The unsupervised learning algorithms are also referred as clustering algorithms. Consider the same case discussed for supervised learning, with apples and tomatoes. Here, the model will take in all images and give out two clusters. One cluster will be "apple" whereas the other cluster will have all the photos of "tomato." When a new image is given to the model, it will be placed in one of the two clusters based on its features.

4.4.3 Reinforcement Learning Algorithm

The reinforcement learning algorithm is a machine learning algorithm, which uses the computer agent to learn the optimal behaviour of the environment and ought to take appropriate actions to achieve the maximum reward. This is mainly about the decision-making process, for which the feedback obtained is crucial. This is a feedback-based learning process. This method of learning is used in most of the robots and computer-based games. Here, the input need not have labeled data. Instead, the model learns by interacting with the environment and receiving feedback from it. The first time the model picks a decision, based on the feedback, the model learns whether its decision is right or wrong. So, this supervised learning relaxes the task of giving completely labeled data for training. A very common example is a computer chess game, if the computer loses while playing with you, then the program will remember all the steps that the player and the system made. Next time, the same strategy won't work in the system and eventually the player will lose to the program.

Oh, does all this seem to be Greek or Latin to you? Don't worry, we will use an example to understand the process.

Let's take a simple example for reinforcement learning. Consider a mom teaching her kid, and, when he makes a mistake, the mom gives feedback which could be helpful to him the very next time (Figure 4.12).

What's this my son?

Input

Mom, it is an orange.

No, My boy, it is Apple.   This is the feedback!

Input

Oh, Apologies mom, I shall correct

What's this my son?

Input

Mom, it is an apple

Figure 4.12   Reinforcement learning.

4.4.4 Evolutionary Approach

This strategy is still evolving and is not an easy one. These types of algorithms imitate natural evolution to solve a particular problem. For instance, genetic algorithms can be employed to solve a problem. This is beyond the scope of this book and hence is ignored for now.

4.5 So, Why Do We Need ML?

This is a wonderful question, at the right time. By this time, it is obvious that we use our own experience to learn things. Say, for a simple example, going back to childhood. Yes, childhood is a treasure chest full of experiences, right? So, why not take another example?!

Do you ever remember the very first time your hand got hurt toughing a hot vessel in the kitchen? Unless that was a big accident, no one usually even remembers that instance? However, now you are old, do you still need somebody's assistance to understand whether a vessel is hot, and you shouldn't touch it? Here, you could understand the experiential learning. Maybe, when you were a kid, you would have touched a hot pot and instantly you would have got the impulse. That feedback stays in your collective memory and, whenever you see a pot, you just take a precaution to determine whether it is hot or not.

Yes, we humans have intelligence to do all of these things. But we cannot reach everywhere and always do such a sort of things. But we have the intelligence to program a machine to follow our orders. This is exactly what we are trying to do in machine learning. So why do we do all these things? The reason is this will make our lives easy. If we can build an interactive and self-adaptive learning algorithm for a machine and if we could train the machine in the way that we need to achieve things, there is nothing like it. However, everything has its own flaws coming along. As humans, first, we should know where to limit the use of machines and to what extent. Anything and every-thing could be trained for negative intentions, too.

Where humans cannot achieve accuracy, yes, machines could bring it. So, making the machines work using human intelligence is a good strategy. Machines with ML algorithms don't require explicit human intervention, as mentioned earlier, and machines can always adapt to the environment, learn from feedback and avoid repeated mistakes.

4.6 Machine Learning Framework

A machine learning framework has various steps, which use math, tools and techniques. The first step is all about gathering data from alternative relevant sources. It all starts from the data, as data acts as the fuel for the whole process. The next step is basically data cleansing or an extensive exploratory data analysis step, where we need to clean and understand the data as much as possible, as this will help later processes to be smooth, easy and inferential. Building the appropriate model is the next step in the process. Training and testing need to be done. The most important step is understanding the patterns from the results and making the correct inferences for the betterment of the whole process itself. Visualization techniques could be of great help, to identify the hidden golden nuggets of information from the results. This concludes the flow of the ML framework. However, as a picture can speak a thousand words, let's depict the whole process flow as a simple diagrammatic representation (Figure 4.13).

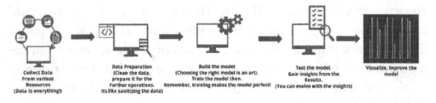

Figure 4.13 Machine learning framework.

4.7 Machine Learning *vs* Deep Learning

We have been talking about machine learning algorithms, their types, framework, etc. Now, it is time to dive a little bit deeper and understand the major differences between ML and DL algorithms. The difference in their process flow can be best understood from Figure 4.14.

4.8 Common Applications of ML

Some of the common ML applications you will have already experienced in your life include:

- FB (Facebook) recommending you friends.
- Amazon recommending you products.
- Flipkart recommending you products.
- Netflix recommendations

Netflix recommends you with the best TV series, based on your taste but based on ML. So, the point is simple. With ML in the picture, a company can identify more opportunities for making good profits. A

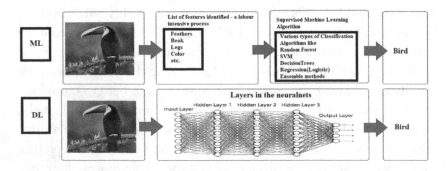

Figure 4.14 Difference in process flow with ML and DL.

scenario: you are browsing about holidays in Thailand. You have not booked any tickets or even confirmed the trip. Upon logging into your Facebook account, you will be receiving the Thailand holiday-related posts. That is ML for you! It helps in finding avenues for new business and enhancing profit for subscribing companies, all without any errors or human intervention. No operator is necessary to link that Thai holiday advertisement to your Facebook page.

Further major application of ML are in:

- *Agricultural sector*: To identify the crop diseases.
- *Energy sector*: To predict the consumption of energy for a region in the next two months.
- *Education sector*: To predict the number of students completing the course and the job openings in the market.
- *Government sector*: Many ML-related applications are used, such as automated identification of the unique Identifier from a captured image of a person, for facial recognition purposes.
- *Other Sectors*: Financial sector, media sector, retail sector, smart home and telecom are some of the other sectors where we frequently employ machine learning concepts.

Well, it was a fascinating chapter, right?! Let's progress further to explore Pandas, Data Frames, and Libraries for visualization. The next chapter awaits you!

Resources

- Vasudevan, S.K., Pulari, S.R., & Vasudevan, S. (2021). Deep Learning: A Comprehensive Guide (1st ed.). Chapman and Hall/CRC Press. https://doi.org/10.1201/9781003185635
- Murphy, K. P. (2012). Machine Learning: A Probabilistic Perspective. Cambridge, MA, MIT Press.
- https://www.youtube.com/playlist?list=PL3uLubnzL2T1 -7fugIeCk4-14HVVdn5_v

4.9 Key Points to Remember

1. Machine learning is a branch of AI, which can help a machine learn and act by imitating intelligent human behaviour.

2. AI is the broader umbrella term, and machine learning and deep learning come under this umbrella. All of them are related to each other.

3. Machine learning algorithms are categorized as supervised learning, unsupervised learning and reinforcement learning. Evolutionary learning algorithms make use of genetic algorithms.

4. Supervised learning algorithms use labeled datasets. They have a training phase to model and a testing phase to predict or classify the data. They are used to handle classification problem.

5. Unsupervised learning algorithms don't not use labeled data; they categorize data into groups or clusters. They are clustering algorithms.

6. Reinforcement learning receives feedback from the environment, using computer agents and actions, to best utilize the parameters for optimal rewards.

7. Machine learning can perform adaptive learning, to bring the greatest accuracy to the process, taking feedback and making the process less error prone, and using them for recurrent tasks.

8. Machine learning frameworks mainly include the following steps: data collection, data analysis, model building, testing the model, visualization and results interpretation.

9. Machine learning uses ML algorithms to predict or classify the data, whereas deep learning (DL) uses neural networks and its hidden layers to provide the output, which makes it a bit harder to understand and find the inferences.

10. Machine learning has many applications in various sectors like retail, agriculture, finance, healthcare, education, energy, government, etc., in addition to Facebook recommending you friends, Amazon and Flipkart recommending you products, Netflix recommending movies, etc.

Quiz Questions (Answer It Yourself, Folks!)

1. What is machine learning?
2. How are AI, ML and DL related?

3. State the types of machine learning algorithms
4. What is supervised learning? Can you explain with an example?
5. What is unsupervised learning? Can you relate with an example?
6. What is reinforcement learning? Can you describe with an example?
7. Why do we need machine learning?
8. Can you elaborate on the machine learning framework?
9. List a few machine learning applications.
10. Describe the differences between a ML and DL process.

5

TOOLS AND PRE-REQUISITES

Learning Objectives

After going through this chapter, the reader should be able to understand the following:

- The basics of Pandas.
- Data frames and operations.
- Visualization tools and options.

5.1 Introduction

This chapter is going to explore Pandas, data frames and libraries for use in output visualization. Python is chosen for many reasons: two good reasons are "resource availability" and "community connect." The reader will learn to understand the concepts through relevant examples and the results presented alongside.

5.2 What's Used in This Chapter?

Readers shall be introduced to the following toolsets in this chapter. They are easy to use and certainly interesting to learn.

- *Jupyter Notebooks*: This is one of the most common tools used today for interactive coding and output visualization, which is easy to use and learn. The same is now integrated with Intel DevCloud, which we have discussed in detail in Chapter 3. The reader can revisit this chapter if needed.
- *NumPy, Pandas*: These are the keys for someone to get the best out of the numerical computations conducted.
- *Matplotlib, Seaborn*: When you talk about output visualization, the simplest and the most effective approach is to use Matplotlib/Seaborn. Both are very well-known and widely used by data scientists all over the world.

DOI: 10.1201/9781003393122-5

This chapter will throw light on all of these, with examples and exercises. Stay tuned. It is time to go practical now.

5.3 Let's Learn Pandas

Well, Pandas is amazing. It is fast, powerful and flexible as well. It is very easy to learn and use. It is an open-source data manipulation and analysis tool which is built over Python. Actually, Pandas is packed with a lot of extremely useful functionalities. Even working with complex data appears easier when you choose Pandas. Most importantly, it is always very much easier to access statistical functions, visualizations, etc. It is fun and this section will enable the reader to understand Pandas. One can visit the official Pandas website @ https://pandas.pydata.org/

Remember this.

Pandas actually is an abbreviation for the Panel Datasets. The data are always referred to in the tabular format which has rows and columns.

5.3.1 Let's Install

It is simple. You need to have Python (latest version) and Anaconda already installed. This will make life easier. Follow the steps presented below and it will help install Pandas with ease.

Go to the Anaconda Prompt (it has to be understood that the Anaconda Prompt is different from the Command Prompt). One could refer to the screenshot presented below in Figure 5.1 which reveals the Anaconda Prompt. If you are using the Intel DevCloud, you can directly install with the Jupyter Notebook through DevCloud.

Figure 5.1 The Anaconda Prompt.

One can launch the Jupyter Notebook with the Command Jupyter Lab through the Anaconda Prompt. One can refer to Figure 5.2 to understand this step, which will enable you to launch the Python Notebook. That's it. You would have gotten the Notebook for you to type your code as shown in Figure 5.3.

As shown in Figure 5.3, just use the command "import pandas" to obtain Pandas for you. You can validate the same with the "pandas.__version__" command. The same can be seen in Figure 5.3.

It's easy!

Now the actual learning starts. One should understand the basic point here. As far as Pandas is concerned, the most common and basic data structure is the "Series." It is the basic building block for the data in tabular format.

5.3.2 What Is a Data Frame?

We need structured data for carrying out all the data analytics. We are familiar with SQL (Structured Query Language), right? It is all about rows and columns and makes life easier.

For Data Science and ML with Python, we have something similar called data frames (the dataset has to be converted to data frames for easier access and processing). Here, the data are being visualized as a table, making interpretation much easier.

Pandas Library will help in getting the data frames created so let's learn the same.

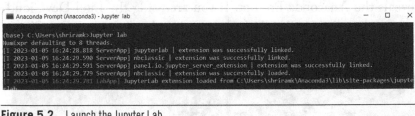

Figure 5.2   Launch the Jupyter Lab.

```
[1]:  import pandas
      pandas.__version__

[1]:  '1.4.4'
```

Figure 5.3   The Notebook.

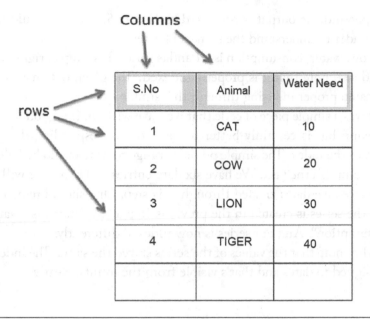

Figure 5.4   A sample data frame (with heterogeneous data inside).

One should remember that the data frame is a 2D data structure. Can we have an example to enhance our understanding? Your first data frame is presented below which will certainly enhance the reader's understanding of the data frame. We will use the data frames at a later point of this chapter, and this is just a head's up for information.

Remember:

- We will come across CSV files in many of our ML/DL projects. A CSV file is a Comma Separated Values (CSV) file and is a plain text file that stores data by delimiting data entries with commas.

5.3.3 Pandas Series Creation and Indexing

We are going to create the Pandas series first. It is very simple, and we need to have data for the same. We are using the water consumption by an apartment as the data, and we shall build the Pandas series around these data. First step is to import the Pandas, which will mostly be imported as pd. Next, one should create an array. Then, the constructor pd series is to be used to get the series created. The code snippet and the output is presented as Figure 5.5, and it would help the reader to understand the scenario better.

Now, water_consumption is a Pandas series. It's simple, right? One could also note that it is properly indexed. The given data have been allocated proper indexing through this simple step.

It was a simple piece of code that we have written. It is good to have indexing but is certainly better to have the corresponding dates in place of the index. The simple pd.date_range routine would be helpful to accomplish the task. We have six data entries and hence we will get six successive dates created through this step. One should remember that the series is created in the previous step and its name is "water_consumption". And our series is now indexed differently.

Also, note that the values of the series stayed the same. The index is reassigned to dates and that's visible from the results, clearly.

5.3.4 Operations with the Series – It's Fun

One can retrieve the values from the series with the index. It is easy and is akin to using a dictionary. One could see the code snippet presented in Figure 5.7 to understand the same.

```
import pandas as pd

water_data = [1000, 1200, 1300,
             1400, 1500, 1600]
water_consumption = pd.Series(water_data,          name='Water_Consumption')
print(water_consumption)

0    1000
1    1200
2    1300
3    1400
4    1500
5    1600
Name: Water_Consumption, dtype: int64
```

Figure 5.5   The first Pandas series.

```
water_consumption.index = pd.date_range('20230101',periods=6)

print(water_consumption)

2023-01-01    1000
2023-01-02    1200
2023-01-03    1300
2023-01-04    1400
2023-01-05    1500
2023-01-06    1600
Freq: D, Name: Water_Consumption, dtype: int64
```

Figure 5.6   Adding date range to the series.

```
# Just like a dictionary
print(water_consumption['2023-01-01'])

1000
```

Figure 5.7   Select the data by index values.

```
# Or by index position--Like an array
print(water_consumption[4])

1500
```

Figure 5.8   Select the data by index position.

The next step is to try with the index position, just like an array. It is also possible. This is not supported by dictionaries. The same is revealed in Figure 5.8.

Slicing works fine as well. Here is an example, presented in Figure 5.9, which will make you understand slicing better. The entire January data will be retrieved and is presented.

A series is very versatile and flexible. It can store integers, floats or strings. One can view with ease the data type it stores with the piece of code shown in Figure 5.10. One can see that the data type is an integer.

You can convert the data type with ease too. One can refer to the code presented in Figure 5.11. The conversion of the existing datatype

```
# Select all of January
print(water_consumption['2023-01'])

2023-01-01    1000
2023-01-02    1200
2023-01-03    1300
2023-01-04    1400
2023-01-05    1500
2023-01-06    1600
Freq: D, Name: Water_Consumption, dtype: int64
```

Figure 5.9   Select the data by slicing.

```
# View the data type
print(water_consumption.dtypes)

int64
```

Figure 5.10   Find the data type.

```
# Convert to a float
water_consumption = water_consumption.astype(float)

# View the data type
print(water_consumption.dtypes)

float64
```

Figure 5.11   Datatype conversion.

to float has been presented below. This is such a flexibility the users get. .astype is a series method that can convert the data type.

Handling missing data is a paramount task with the data. Data imputation is the simplest way experts follow when handling missed data. Imputation is the process of replacing missing data with substituted values and the same is presented in Figure 5.12. Also, the reader could see that NaN (Not a Number) is used in the code. It is the Numpy way of conveying that the data are missing. Series.fillna is a method to fill the missing values with the given value. One can observe that the invalid data are created first and then it is replaced with zeros.

Data frames are to be touched on now and the series will be all done. As discussed already, it is two-dimensional in nature and is a collection of series. Remember that – data frames are a collection of series. Series is all one-dimensional, whereas data frames are two-dimensional. You can refer to Figure 5.1 to understand what a data frame looks like. Simply, it is a table of data. Let's learn the data frames.

First, let's create a dataset. The dataset is in .CSV format. The CSV file (data.csv), which has sample data, is presented below for quicker perusal. This is the dataset. Figure 5.13 has the data and one can view the same.

Shall we create data frame from the dataset? Figure 5.14 has the screenshot which shows the way to create the data frame. The file which contains the data is named data.csv and the same is used below to create the data frame.

It's time to understand how the data frame can be visualized. The first few entries of the data frame are all displayed with the piece of code snippet below. df.head (5) will display the first five entries in the data frame.

```
# Create invalid data
water_consumption[1:3] = np.NaN

# Now fill it in with zeros
water_consumption = water_consumption.fillna(0.)
# equivalently,
# step_counts.fillna(0., inplace=True)

print(water_consumption[1:3])

2023-01-02    0.0
2023-01-03    0.0
Freq: D, Name: Water_Consumption, dtype: float64
```

Figure 5.12   Imputation.

A	B	C
animal	ID	water_Need
Elephant	1	100
Tiger	2	200
Lion	3	300
Zebra	4	400
Kangroo	5	500
Pig	6	600
Dog	7	700
Donkey	8	800
Horse	9	900
Cat	10	1000
Cheetah	11	1200
Bee	12	1
Ant	13	1
Crow	14	3

Figure 5.13   The data set (data.csv).

```
import pandas as pd
Animal_DataFrame_df=pd.read_csv ('C:\Ana\ML_Playlist\data.csv')
```

Figure 5.14   The data frame creation.

```
In [11]: import pandas as pd
         Animal_DataFrame_df=pd.read_csv ('C:\Ana\ML_Playlist\data.csv')
         pd.set_option('display.max_columns', 5)
         Animal_DataFrame_df.head(5)
         #Head = Displays the first few rows
         #Set_option (display.max_columns) - Enables you to specify max columns you wanna display!

Out[11]:
           animal  ID  water_Need
         0 Elephant  1      100
         1    Tiger  2      200
         2     Lion  3      300
         3    Zebra  4      400
         4  Kangroo  5      500
```

Figure 5.15   The head – first few entries displayed

It is simple to get a quick summary of the data frame. The list will help us in getting the summary as presented in Figure 5.16.

The transposing operation can be done with ease with transpose() operation. One can see that the transpose operation is completed by transposing Columns as Rows and Rows as Columns, and this is

```
In [16]:  import pandas as pd
          Animal_DataFrame_df=pd.read_csv ('C:\Ana\ML_Playlist\data.csv')
          list(Animal_DataFrame_df.columns)
          # Use Columns attributes to get the summary of columns.

Out[16]:  ['animal', 'ID', 'water_Need']

  In [ ]:
```

Figure 5.16   The list to obtain the summary.

presented below in Figure 5.17. One can view the original data before transpose from Figure 5.13.

One can find the dimensions of the data frame easily with the below piece of code.

The slicing options are interesting too. Slicing is easy with the data frames. One can see how easily the slicing has been enabled with the data frames as shown in Figure 5.19. It sliced the first three entries and we received the output.

One can slice in the reverse order too and this is demonstrated in Figure 5.20 for quicker reference.

It is easy to obtain the occurrence count for each data entry in the data frame through the Pandas. The method value_counts() help in accomplishing this task. One can see the way this is implemented from Figure 5.21.

```
In [1]:  import pandas as pd
         Animal_DataFrame_df=pd.read_csv ('C:\Ana\ML_Playlist\data.csv')
         Animal_DataFrame_df.head(5).transpose()

Out[1]:
```

	0	1	2	3	4
animal	Elephant	Tiger	Lion	Zebra	Kangroo
ID	1	2	3	4	5
water_Need	100	200	300	400	500

Figure 5.17   Transpose operation.

```
In [5]:  Animal_DataFrame_df=pd.read_csv ('C:\Ana\ML_Playlist\data.csv')
         Animal_DataFrame_df.shape

Out[5]:  (15, 3)
```

Figure 5.18   Dimensions of the data frame.

```
In [9]:   Animal_DataFrame_df=pd.read_csv ('C:\Ana\ML_Playlist\data.csv')
          Animal_DataFrame_df[0:3]
```

Out[9]:

	animal	ID	water_Need
0	Elephant	1	100
1	Tiger	2	200
2	Lion	3	300

Figure 5.19 Slicing.

```
In [11]:  Animal_DataFrame_df=pd.read_csv ('C:\Ana\ML_Playlist\data.csv')
          Animal_DataFrame_df[-2:]
```

Out[11]:

	animal	ID	water_Need
13	Crow	14	3
14	Eagle	15	5

Figure 5.20 Slicing backward.

```
In [15]:  Animal_DataFrame_df=pd.read_csv ('C:\Ana\ML_Playlist\data.csv')
          Animal_DataFrame_df.animal.value_counts()
```

```
Out[15]:  Bee        1
          Pig        1
          Donkey     1
          Crow       1
          Elephant   1
          Cheetah    1
          Lion       1
          Zebra      1
          Dog        1
          Kangroo    1
          Eagle      1
          Tiger      1
          Ant        1
          Cat        1
          Horse      1
          Name: animal, dtype: int64
```

Figure 5.21 Count occurrences.

To filter and obtain the results, Pandas provide an easier option. One can see the filtered results presented based on the water_need being more than 10 as shown in Figure 5.22.

If someone wants to remove a column or a row from the data frame, it is also easy.

Initially, the data frame has four columns. To remove a specific column, one should include the name of the column to be removed with the axis described as 1 as shown below in the code snippet presented

```
In [20]:  Animal_DataFrame_df=pd.read_csv ('C:\Ana\ML_Playlist\data.csv')
          Animal_DataFrame_df[Animal_DataFrame_df['water_Need']> 10 ]
```

Out[20]:

	animal	ID	water_Need
0	Elephant	1	100
1	Tiger	2	200
2	Lion	3	300
3	Zebra	4	400
4	Kangroo	5	500
5	Pig	6	600
6	Dog	7	700
7	Donkey	8	800
8	Horse	9	900
9	Cat	10	1000
10	Cheetah	11	1200

Figure 5.22   Filtering.

as Figure 5.23. The output presented does not have the column ID included.

Similarly, one can remove a specific row too; for that to be done, axis should be described as 0 and the row index mentioned. The below code snippet below (Figure 5.24) and the results obtained shall help the reader to understand the same. Here, one can note that Row 2 (Lion) is removed.

That's enough about the data frames – it is time to learn visualizations. Yes, it is important.

5.4 Let's Visualize

Data or results without understanding won't provide any useful insights. Proper visualization will enable the users to gain useful insights. "Image speaks more than words" is a saying and it holds 100% true for data analytics!

```
In [38]:  Animal_DataFrame_df=pd.read_csv ('C:\Ana\ML_Playlist\data.csv')
          # Removing a column - The column name to be mentioned, axis = 1
          Animal_DataFrame_df.drop('ID', inplace = True, axis = 1)
          list(Animal_DataFrame_df.columns)

Out[38]:  ['animal', 'water_Need']
```

Figure 5.23   Removal of the columns from the data frame.

```
In [39]:  # Removing a row - Row index and Axis is to be set as 0
          Animal_DataFrame_df.drop(2, inplace = True, axis = 0)
          Animal_DataFrame_df.head(5)
```

Out[39]:

	animal	water_Need
0	Elephant	100
1	Tiger	200
3	Zebra	400
4	Kangroo	500
5	Pig	600

Figure 5.24　Removal of the rows from the data frame.

This is the most exciting part of learning. Output visualizations can be created in multiple ways, such as matplotlib and seaborn.

- Matplotlib is one of the main libraries used to create plots and graphs. It has so many features. Matplotlib is a comprehensive library for creating static, animated and interactive visualizations in Python. Since Pandas offer very easy-to-use and convenient wrappers around the matplotlib's APIs, it is easier for someone to get the plots created.
- Seaborn is a Python data visualization library based on matplotlib. It provides a high-level interface for drawing attractive and informative statistical graphics.

What is the first step? Well, it is to import and one can understand how we have imported matplotlib and seaborn with the piece of code shown in Figure 5.25.

Figure 5.25　Importing matplotlib and seaborn. Note: seaborn is now "sea," matplotlib is "plot" for the reader.

The same animal dataset shown before in this chapter is further enhanced to a bigger one. One can refer to Figure 5.13 to visualize the earlier version and to Figure 5.26 to understand the enhancements.

a. *Bar Chart – Let's Start Here*: A bar chart is a figure that presents categorical data with rectangular bars with heights or lengths proportional to the values that they represent.

The bars can be plotted vertically or horizontally. Can we present the bar chart now through a simple piece of code? One can see that the bar chart plotting shown for the dataset considered is clear. Sea.barplot method is sufficient to get a clear visualization.

The same can be done with the Hue. One can visualize the same in Figure 5.28.

b. *Histogram*: Histogram is a graphical display of data using bars of different heights. It is similar to a Bar Chart, but a histogram groups numbers into ranges. One can understand the

	A	B	C	D	E
1	Animal	Kg_Val	Animal_IC	Water_Re	Index
2	Elephant	1000	1	200	1
3	Tiger	200	2	15	2
4	Lion	230	3	13	3
5	Zebra	120	4	12	4
6	Kangroo	100	5	18	5
7	Pig	121	6	4	6
8	Dog	45	7	2	7
9	Donkey	588	8	3	8
10	Horse	677	9	6	9
11	Cat	21	10	1	11
12	Cheetah	767	11	20	12
13	Bee	1	12	0.5	13
14	Ant	12	13	0.3	14
15	Crow	2	14	1.5	15
16	Eagle	35	15	2.5	16

Figure 5.26   Extended dataset.

way to get the histogram and what the plot looks like from the bar code snippet and output shown in Figure 5.29.

As an extension, one can get the histograms with a bin. A bin in a histogram is the block (or grouping) that you use to combine values before obtaining the frequency. For instance,

```
In [3]: import matplotlib.pyplot as plot
        import seaborn as  sea
        %matplotlib inline
        import pandas as pd
        Animal_DataFrame_df=pd.read_csv ('C:\Ana\ML_Playlist\data.csv')
        # Let us draw a barchart now! Call the function barplot () from seaborn library
        # Remember seaborn is imported as sea.
        sea.barplot (x='Kg_Val', y='Water_Reqd', data=Animal_DataFrame_df)
        # data should be nothing but your DataFrame!!
```

```
Out[3]: <matplotlib.axes._subplots.AxesSubplot at 0x190e777c988>
```

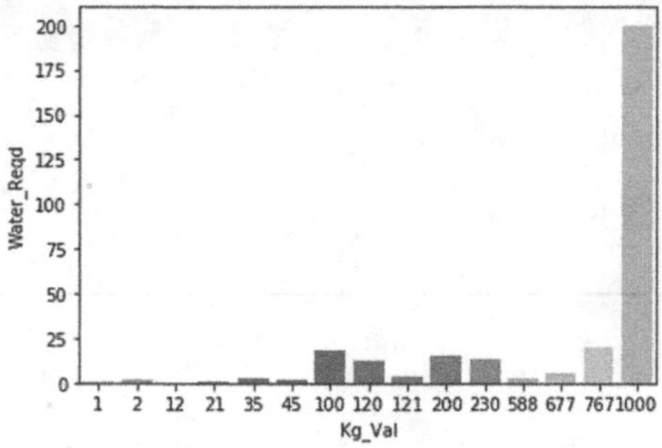

Figure 5.27 Bar chart.

```
In [4]: # With Hue
        import matplotlib.pyplot as plot
        import seaborn as  sea
        %matplotlib inline
        import pandas as pd
        Animal_DataFrame_df=pd.read_csv ('C:\Ana\ML_Playlist\data.csv')
        # Let us draw a barchart now! Call the function barplot () from seaborn library
        # Remember seaborn is imported as sea.
        sea.barplot (x='Kg_Val', y='Water_Reqd', hue='Animal_ID', data=Animal_DataFrame_df)
        # hue can take up the third value and present it nicely for you to visualize!
        # its game
```

```
Out[4]: <matplotlib.axes._subplots.AxesSubplot at 0x190e785e648>
```

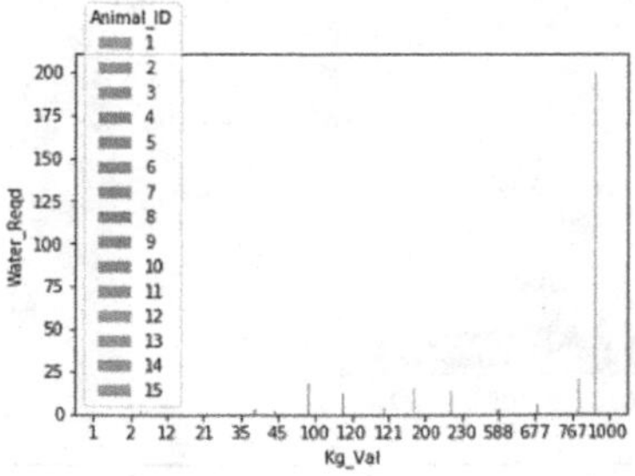

Figure 5.28 Bar chart with Hue.

if you are creating a histogram of age, the bins might be 0–5,
6–10, 11–15, and so on up to 85 and so on. One can refer to
Figure 5.30 to understand the concept better.

c. *Density Plot*: A density plot visualizes the distribution of
data over a continuous interval or time period. This chart is

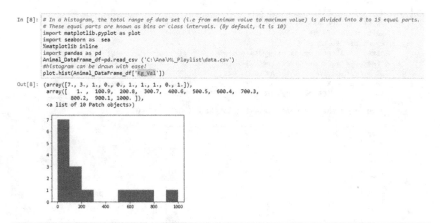

Figure 5.29   The histogram.

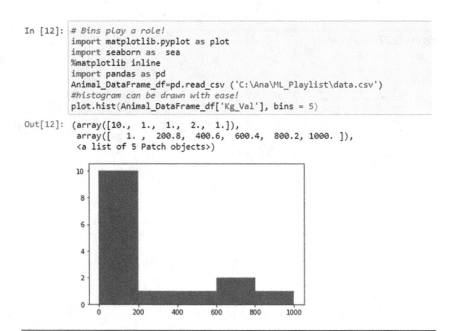

Figure 5.30   The histogram with binning.

a variation of a histogram that obtains smoother distribution by smoothing out the noise. The peaks of a density plot help display the values that are concentrated over the interval. The code snippet and the density plot developed from it is presented as Figure 5.31 for the reader's quicker perusal.

d. *Box Plot*: A box plot is the visual representation of the statistical five-number summary of a given dataset. A five-number summary includes: # minimum, first quartile, median (second quartile), third quartile, maximum. One can visualize what it looks like from Figure 5.32, where the code snippet is also presented.

e. *Scatter Plot*: This helps in revealing the relationship between two variables through the plot. import matplotlib.pyplot as plot. Can we see the code? (refer to Figure 5.33).

f. *Pair Plot*: When you have a need to compare many variables, a pair plot is the best choice. One can see how simple it is to code and obtain good results (Figure 5.34).

```
In [13]:  # Density Plot.
          # this is an enhanced histogram people call.
          # Presents distribution of data over a continuous interval of time.
          import matplotlib.pyplot as plot
          import seaborn as sea
          %matplotlib inline
          import pandas as pd
          Animal_DataFrame_df=pd.read_csv ('C:\Ana\ML_Playlist\data.csv')
          #histogram can be drawn with ease!
          sea.distplot(Animal_DataFrame_df['Kg_Val'])
```

Out[13]: <matplotlib.axes._subplots.AxesSubplot at 0x190e8bec848>

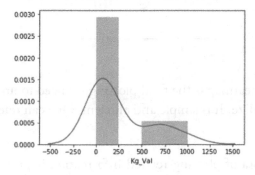

Figure 5.31   The density plot.

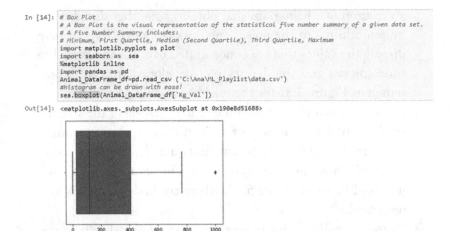

```
In [14]:  # Box Plot
          # A Box Plot is the visual representation of the statistical five number summary of a given data set.
          # A Five Number Summary includes:
          # Minimum, First Quartile, Median (Second Quartile), Third Quartile, Maximum
          import matplotlib.pyplot as plot
          import seaborn as sea
          %matplotlib inline
          import pandas as pd
          Animal_DataFrame_df=pd.read_csv ('C:\Ana\ML_Playlist\data.csv')
          #histogram can be drawn with ease!
          sea.boxplot(Animal_DataFrame_df['Kg_Val'])

Out[14]:  <matplotlib.axes._subplots.AxesSubplot at 0x190e8d51688>
```

Figure 5.32   The box plot.

```
In [15]:  # Scatter Plot
          # This helps in revealing the relationship between two variables through the plot.
          import matplotlib.pyplot as plot
          import seaborn as  sea
          %matplotlib inline
          import pandas as pd
          Animal_DataFrame_df=pd.read_csv ('C:\Ana\ML_Playlist\data.csv')
          # Scatter Plot.
          plot.scatter (x = Animal_DataFrame_df.Kg_Val, y = Animal_DataFrame_df.Animal_ID)

Out[15]:  <matplotlib.collections.PathCollection at 0x190e8e71588>
```

Figure 5.33   The scatter plot.

g. *Heatmap*: The heatmap is the final plotting we need to understand and visualize. It is simple and efficient. One can refer to Figure 5.35.

That's it! The plethora of plotting-related information is provided to the reader. It's time for the reader to start to practice. Ready, Get Set, Pandas!

In [16]:
```
import matplotlib.pyplot as plot
import seaborn as sea
%matplotlib inline
import pandas as pd
Animal_DataFrame_df=pd.read_csv ('C:\Ana\ML_Playlist\data.csv')
# Scatter Plot.
features = ['Kg_Val', 'Animal_ID', 'Water_Reqd']
sea.pairplot (Animal_DataFrame_df [features])
# Here many variables are compared! Its easy!
```

Out[16]: <seaborn.axisgrid.PairGrid at 0x190e8e3c6c8>

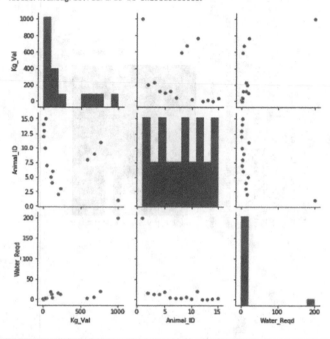

Figure 5.34   The pair plot.

We hope you readers enjoy learning the contents of this chapter. Supervised learning awaits you in the next chapter. Let's carry on!

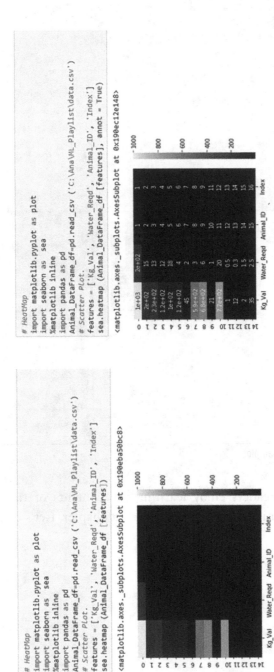

Figure 5.35 The heatmap.

Resources

- https://youtu.be/bzaO9SFHJSA
- https://youtu.be/VnkfaI9tG4M
- https://youtu.be/xXOPfrba8I0
- https://pandas.pydata.org/
- https://seaborn.pydata.org/
- https://matplotlib.org/

5.5 Key Points to Remember

- One of the most common tools used today for interactive coding and visualization of output is the Jupyter Notebook.
- NumPy and Pandas are the key for the reader to get the best of the numerical computations carried out.
- The simplest and the most effective approach to visualization is to use Matplotlib/Seaborn.
- Pandas is fast, powerful, and flexible as well. It is very easy to learn and use. It is open-source data manipulation and analysis tool which is built above python.
- Pandas is an abbreviation for the Panel Datasets. The data are always referred to in the tabular format which has rows and columns.
- Operations with the Pandas series are very easy and fun.
- Handling missing data is a paramount task with the data. Data imputation is the simplest way which experts follow to handle missing data. Imputation is the process of replacing missing data with substituted values.
- Data visualization is an important aspect of data analytics. Matplotlib and Seaborn provide you with support for better visualization experiences.

6

SUPERVISED LEARNING

Learning Objectives

After reading this chapter, the reader should be able to understand the following:

- What is supervised learning?
- Types of supervised learning algorithms.
- What is regression?
- Where is regression useful?
- Steps in regression.
- Implementation of regression.
- Logistic regression.
- Linear *vs* logistic regression.
- What is classification?
- K-nearest neighbors (KNN) – steps.
- Implementation of KNN.
- Loss and cost function, bias and variance trade-off, regularization, feature selection, hyperparameter tuning.

6.1 Introduction

So, we are back to square one, with the concept of supervised learning. If anyone has skipped Chapter 4, we highly recommend you to take some time to go through the real-time examples of supervised learning and then head toward this chapter.

Supervised learning algorithms take a dataset, build a model using the training dataset and validate them using the test dataset and predict or classify the results. The accuracy of the model can be calculated so that we can have a good understanding of the model that we have used for prediction or classification purposes. If required, we can also have feedback to improve the process.

 DOI: 10.1201/9781003393122-6

6.2 Types of Supervised Learning Algorithms

Supervised learning algorithms are mainly categorized as regression algorithms and classification algorithms (Figure 6.1). An email spam classifier is an example of a classification algorithm.

6.2.1 Classification

Supervised learning, as you will know by now, can be seen employed quite often in our day-to-day lives. Will there be a single person who doesn't open his Gmail inbox in a day? Even our kids need Gmail access for accessing Google classrooms. The inbox of Gmail is bombarded with advertisements and spam emails. Yes, I am coming to this spam classifier (Figure 6.2). If Gmail didn't offer this spam classification, I couldn't even imagine how many more emails I would have to manually classify. Hence, when we look around, we use supervised learning algorithms knowingly or unknowingly.

The major intention of this chapter is to introduce you with the various types of supervised learning algorithms. We mainly focus on regression and classification. This chapter is not comprehensive as these are very large topics with lots of research being carried out. However, we will strive to make you understand how to implement simple linear regression and simple KNN classification algorithms. Only when we make our hands dirty, will we learn more! Isn't that true? Yes, come on, let's dive in together for a deeper learning experience.

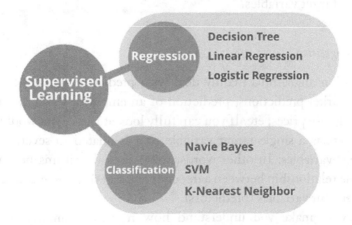

Figure 6.1 Types of supervised learning algorithms.

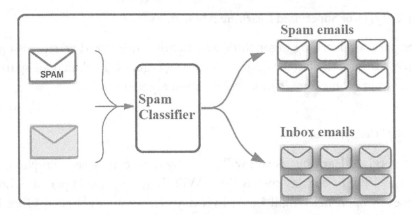

Figure 6.2 Spam email classifier.

Say you have always noticed how your parents were busy making ends meet and following the traditional dreams laid out by society (at least a few parents☺). They might be always busy making money for your fees and the ultimate goal for all parents is to own a house. You may have noticed at one stage, when they decided to buy a house, that they were calling all the broker agents, going to the house/land sites directly and making enquiries to neighbors to pay the best price for the plot where they are looking to build their dream house. At times, if the parents are busy, they will finally decide to buy an already-built house. However, if we had our way, house price prediction would have been a great help for our parents. This is actually an example for regression, where we deal with continuous target variables.

6.2.2 Regression

Regression algorithms mainly deal with predictive applications like stock market predictions, prediction of an employee's salary, prediction of house prices, etc. If you carefully look at these, you would find that there is a single target variable that is related to several independent variables. In other words, regression algorithms help us to find the relationship between a dependent (target) variable and several independent variables (predictors).

Now to make you understand how regression analysis is part of supervised learning, keeping in mind that regression analysis starts with a dataset where the target attribute is known or labeled. Supervised learning is thus based on labeled data.

To make it clear, say, when the variable of a dataset is completely numerical and the target variable is numerical, then the regression analysis will predict a number. For example, a regression model can predict house prices, if we have observations of houses over a certain period of time. House variables may include house area (square meters), number of bedrooms, number of bathrooms, garage space, number of floors, building materials, close proximity to resources such as schools, shops, facilities, etc. which are the independent predictors. Regression model predicts the target variable – house price – based on the linear relationship between house price and a combination of these predictors.

6.3 Applications Where Regression Is Useful?

6.3.1 Trend Analysis

Regression is mainly useful in application areas like trend analysis. Have you ever used Google Trends? If not, it is something which has to be tried for sure. Google Trends brings in the most popular search query trends and is mainly used by forecasters and academics for prediction-based analyses. The major data used by Google Trends are the daily searches people make in the Google search engine. The main plus point is that it can locate outliers or irregular spam search activity. Google trends analyses operate by regression modeling, while searching for join points.

During the recently concluded 2022 FIFA Men's World Cup event, you could imagine the search trends of the word "World Cup"; this basically works by regression analysis, using one of the techniques listed below (Figure 6.3).

Figure 6.3 Google trends for the search query "World Cup" (day-wise and region-wise analysis results).

6.3.2 *Time Series Prediction*

A time series is a collection of values or observations of data gathered over a period of time through repeated measurements. Time series prediction or forecasting use regression analysis widely for predicting future values. Economic and sales forecasting, budgetary analysis, stock market analysis, yield projections, process and quality control, inventory studies, temperature predictions, etc., are all examples of time series predictions that could be done by using regression analysis (Figure 6.4).

6.3.3 *Biomedical Imaging*

Regression techniques are commonly useful in the medical imaging and radiology fields of research. They allow identification of the relationship between the various independent parameters for determining the target variable. Multiple regression analysis is basically used to predict disease progression from the data available in electronic format. Normally the regression analysis is widely used for evaluating the results gathered from visual grading experiments like medical images from radiological studies (Figure 6.5).

6.4 Types of Regression

Now that we know about regression and its most common applications, the major job left is to understand the various steps involved in the regression process. Yes, this is a good start. However, it is important to know that there are different types of regression too. Oh my God, are you kidding me?! Not at all. The big brains who found the

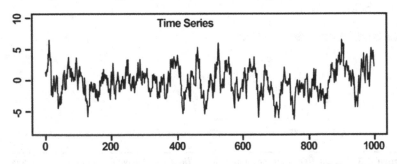

Figure 6.4   Time series graph showing the trend of stock.

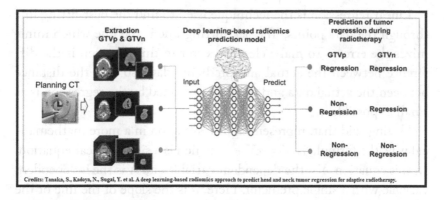

Extraction GTVp & GTVn
Deep learning-based radiomics prediction model
Prediction of tumor regression during radiotherapy

Planning CT

Input
Predict

GTVp
GTVn

Regression
Regression

Non-Regression
Regression

Non-Regression
Non-Regression

Credits: Tanaka, S., Kadoya, N., Sugai, Y. et al. A deep learning-based radiomics approach to predict head and neck tumor regression for adaptive radiotherapy.

Figure 6.5 Medical imaging using regression analysis.

regression analysis have come up with various types of regression. Let's have a quick look into the types now. Don't worry, we'll keep things simple and easily understandable.

- *Linear regression* (a predictive technique, but not classification; classification is used for categorical variables, whereas linear regression uses numerical variables which are of the continuous type).
- *Logistic regression* (a classification technique, because it is used for categorical variables, which are of a discrete, discontinuous type).
- Oh, that was quite simple! Right?
- OK, anyway, let's deep dive into the steps involved in linear regression.

6.4.1 Linear Regression and the Steps Involved

Simple linear regression is a simple technique used to find the relationship between one dependent variable and one or more independent variables. That is, simply stated, regression analysis tries to establish a clear relationship between the input and output.

The dependent variable [target variable] = Output

The independent variables [Predictors] = Input

Linear regression is the technique used to find the best-fitting line through the data points. The best-fitting line is the line which minimizes the errors. To make clear, an error in this situation is the difference between the actual and predicted data, so that the distance between the actual data and the data predicted by the regression is as small as possible.

Having said that, representing the situation in a more mathematical way, the formula is $Y = aX + b$, which is a simple linear equation. In this equation, Y is the dependent variable and X is the independent variable with a single predictor. Here, a is the slope of the line or the regression coefficient and b is the intercept. Regression is a statistical tool to predict the dependent variable with the help of one or more independent variables (multiple predictors).

$b = \bar{y} - a\bar{x}$, where b is the intercept

$$a = \frac{\sum(x_i - \bar{x})(y_i - \bar{y})}{\sum(x_i - \bar{x})^2}, \textit{where a is the slope}$$

Let's take a very familiar example to understand this. We all might have experienced the scenario of studying the day before a test/exam and passing the test the very next day. If you haven't experienced this in your student life, we could say you have missed the training for some major employability skills in your life ☺.

The problem is simple: predict whether the student will pass the exam or not, depending on the numbers of hours spent studying.

Here, the linear regression line draws a relationship between the independent variable and the dependent variable (Figure 6.6).

Case 1 – Positive Relationship
What will be the situation as the independent variable changes? When the independent variable increases, if the dependent variable also increases, we call the relationship (and, hence, the regression) positive (Figure 6.7 and Figure 6.8).

See the picture below:

Here, there is a positive relationship.

- x = number of hours spent studying
- y = passed the test.

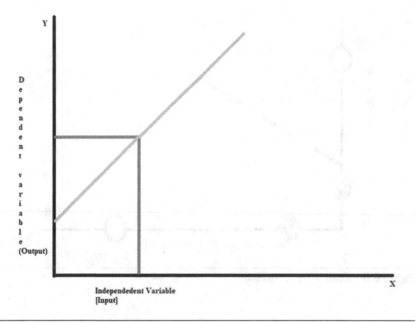

Figure 6.6 Linear regression line.

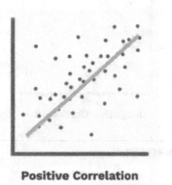

Positive Correlation

Figure 6.7 A Positive correlation.

If y increases positively as x increases, it is called positive relationship. In this case, the number of hours studied increases, which increases the probability of passing the test.

The next regression to learn is the negative relationship. One could look at Figure 6.9 to understand what the negative relationship is all about.

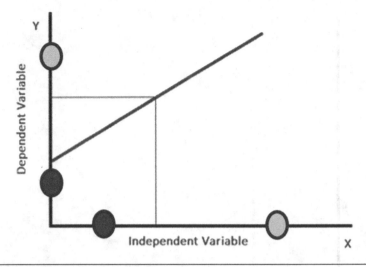

Figure 6.8 A positive linear regression.

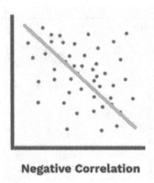

Negative Correlation

Figure 6.9 A negative linear regression.

Case 2 – Negative Relationship

When the independent variable increases and the dependent variable decreases, we call that a negative relationship.

x = number of hours spent watching TV.

y = decrease in CGPA(Cumulative Grade Point Average - for schools and colleges, CGPA is used to measure the overall academic achievement of a student by awarding relevant grades)

If y decreases as x increases, it is called a negative relationship. In this case, the CGPA decreases as the number of hours of TV watched increases. One could also look at Figure 6.10.

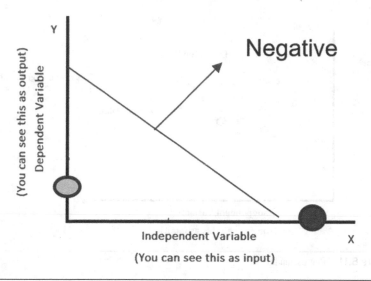

Figure 6.10   A negative linear relationship.

With the simple linear regression, one would aim to drawing a straight line through the *x*, *y* data points. (Regressions can be used to analyze non-linear relationships can still, though that will not be covered in this book.) We plot each of the *x*, *y* pair of observations as dots. Then a straight line has to be drawn that fits all the different points as closely as possible (i.e., with minimal error) and it is called the Regression line. This is drawn using the Least Squares method. The core aim is to minimize the error by means of drawing the regression line. A regression line is presented in Figure 6.11 and one can understand the purpose of this clearly now.

One can also follow the video lecture presented at the YouTube link which talks about the Linear Regression: https://youtu.be/MdHe7Sn6Qt4

To understand what the errors are all about, one can have a look at Figure 6.12.

The overall aim of the regression is to reduce the error to as low as possible. It is time to go with a little mathematics now. Readers must be familiar with these fundamental mathematical terminologies already and, in that case, it would be a recap for those readers. Otherwise, it is important to pay attention to the next couple of sections where it is all fairly fundamental mathematics.

One should refer to Figure 6.13 before getting into the expressions presented below.

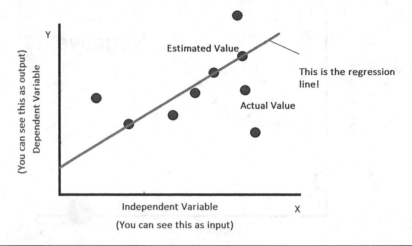

Figure 6.11 Regression line.

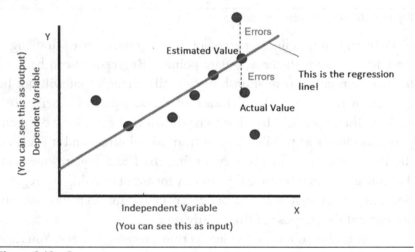

Figure 6.12 Errors.

One should recollect the $Y = MX + C$ expression to describe a straight line, which was learnt during schooldays. This will come in handy here.

$$Y = b_0 + b_1 * x$$

- Y = estimated Pay
- x = number of hours worked
- b_0 = y intercept
- b_1 = slope of the line – here, there is a positive relationship and hence the equation includes "$+b_1$"

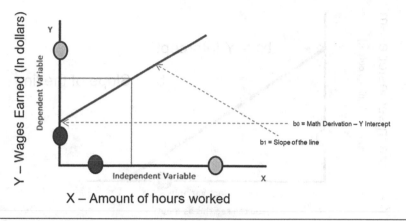

Figure 6.13 The mathematical connect – positive impact.

As the number of hours worked increases, the pay should increase. Hence, there is a positive relationship.

- x is the independent variable which alone can be controlled.
- y is the dependent variable and is the outcome. The salary is dependent on the number of hours worked. (This variable is fully dependent)

$$Y = b_0 - b_1 * x$$

- Y = CGPA
- x = number of hours watching TV
- b_0 = y intercept
- b_1 = slope of the line. There is a negative impact and hence is "$-b_1$"

As the number of hours watching TV increases, the CGPA score will come down. Hence, there is a negative relationship (see Figure 6.14).

- x is the independent variable. Y is the dependent variable and is the outcome.

The next step is to understand how to calculate the linear regression derived using the Least Squares Method. This is one of the most commonly used approaches for linear regression calculation/plotting.

The first step is to create a simple dataset. The entire process is presented step by step:

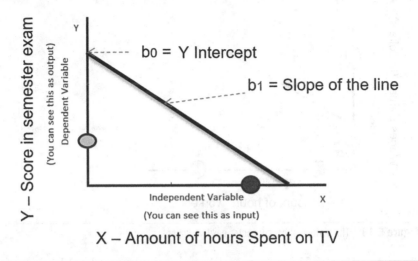

X – Amount of hours Spent on TV

Figure 6.14   The mathematical connect – negative impact

- *Step 1:* x is the input and y is the output. x can be termed the independent Variable and y the dependent variable (see Table 6.1). For each of the five x values, there is one corresponding y value. Collect the pairs of x/y values.

The immediate next step is to calculate mean x and mean y.

$$\text{Mean } x = (1 + 2 + 3 + 4 + 5) / 5 = 3.$$

$$\text{Mean } y = (2 + 4 + 6 + 3 + 5)/ 5 = 4.$$

So, we have calculated the mean x and mean y values. It is time for the reader to go to the next step in the sequence. Can we draw a plot of the relationship, by plotting the five values of the independent variable against the corresponding five values of the dependent variable (Figure 6.15).

One can look at Figure 6.16 to understand how the plotting is done.

Table 6.1   The Data Points

X	Y
1	2
2	4
3	6
4	3
5	5

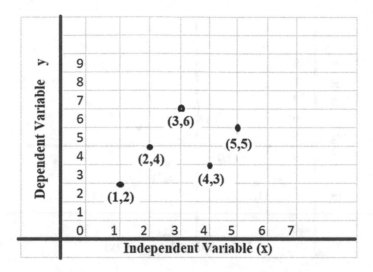

Figure 6.15 Plot of *x vs y*.

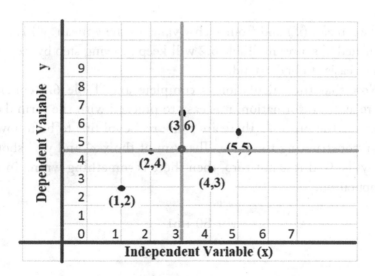

Figure 6.16 Mean *x* and mean *y* plot.

The next step is to calculate the slope and the y intercept (intercept of the line on the y axis) plotted. It is to be taken forward from the previously presented graph shown in Figure 6.17.

The above plots have allowed the visualization of the data in the form of a graph and it is mandatory to visualize the data points in an understandable manner. Now, we need to calculate the distance from each data point to the line-of-best-fit. The distance from each x value

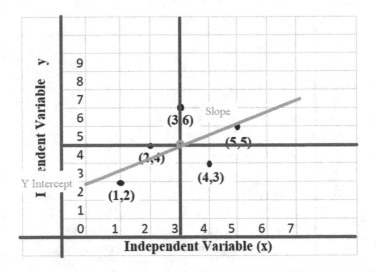

Figure 6.17　*Y* intercept and the slope.

to the x mean (x') and from each y value to the y mean (y') is to be calculated. As a result, Table 6.2 will keep growing step by step and will be easier to understand.

Now that the calculation is complete and Table 6.2 contains the required information, it is easy to proceed with the formula to complete the process. There are some real cool tips to be followed when constructing the table. The sum of the x-x' and y-y' should always be 0; if it is not zero, then there is something wrong in the computation.

$$y' = b0 + b1 * x'$$

$$b1 = 5 / 10 = 0.5$$

Table 6.2　The Data Points

X	Y	X - X'	Y - Y'	(X-X')²	(X-X') (Y-Y')
1	2	$1 - 3 = -2$	$2 - 4 = -2$	4	$-2 \times -2 = 4$
2	4	$2 - 3 = -1$	$4 - 4 = 0$	1	$-1 \times 0 = 0$
3	6	$3 - 3 = 0$	$6 - 4 = 2$	0	$0 \times 2 = 0$
4	3	$4 - 3 = 1$	$3 - 4 = -1$	1	$1 \times -1 = -1$
5	5	$5 - 3 = 2$	$5 - 4 = 1$	4	$1 \times 2 = 2$
				10	5

The above is derived through the expression:

$$b1 = \Sigma\,[(x - x') \, (y - y')] \,/\, \Sigma(x - x^2)$$

where Σ=summation.

We are into the final stage of the computation.

$$y' = b0 + b1 \cdot x'$$

(x' and y' are the mean x and mean y, respectively)

$4 = b0 + b1*3$

$4 = b0 + 0.5 * 3$

$4 = b0 + 1.5$

$4 - 1.5 = b0 + 1.5 - 1.5$

$b0 = 2.5$

$b1 = slope = 0.5$

$b0 = y$ intercept $= 2.5$

So, you have now calculated how to draw the straight regression line ("line-of-best-fit"), which will pass through x'/y' and x=0/y=2.5 (when x=0, the intercept on the y axis is 2.5).

The time has now come for us to learn what exactly the logistic regression is. The terminologies of logistic and linear regressions are very important and they are among the most discussed topics in machine learning.

6.4.2 Logistic Regression – A Sneak Peek

A logistic regression is a mathematical model, which predicts the probability of the occurrence of y, given the information of x, a previous event. Given x, the logistic regression predicts whether y will occur or not. Logistic regression is a binary event, which means y can be either 0 or 1. y gets the value 1, if the event occurs, whereas y gets the value 0 if the event does not occur.

Logistic regression is mainly used for classification applications like spam email detection, diabetes/cancer detection for a person based on various features provided, etc. Another popular application is customer choice prediction – i.e., whether the customer will click on a particular link or not. Will the customer buy the product or not?

6.4.3 Comparison of Linear and Logistic Regressions

Linear regression gives you a continuous variable output, but logistic regression provides a discrete variable output. Linear regression illustrates a straight-line relationship but logistic regression deals with a relationship following a sigmoidal function.

Briefly:

- Linear regression is an approach to model the linear relationship between dependent and independent variables.
- Logistic regression is more statistical in nature where the model predicts the outcome which could be one of the two values.

Learning or implementing logistic and linear regression through codes is beyond the scope of this book. But, the authors have provided a clear video lecture for the reader who wants to explore the implementation aspects as well.

Implementation of Linear Regression: https://youtu.be/i6G94Me9LN0

Implementation of Logistic Regression: https://youtu.be/snr1q_iq-bE

It is time to understand what classification is all about.

6.4.4 Implementation of Linear Regression

As discussed, linear regression is one of the most important and best-known algorithms. Having explained the theory behind linear regression earlier in this chapter, it is time for the reader to understand how the same can be implemented.

- *Step 1:* It is important to do the necessary imports. The code is made available in the https://github.com/shriramkv/MachineLearningwithoneAPI for quick reference. The necessary importing has to be done from the below code.

```
import numpy as np
import matplotlib.pyplot as plt
import joblib
import random
import time

from sklearnex import patch_sklearn, unpatch_sklearn
```

- *Step 2:* The next step is to ensure the Intel optimized sklearn is used and, for that to be done, patch_sklearn is used with the piece of code below. To highlight how Intel-optimized sklearn can be used for building linear regression models, the emphasis is made. One can also confirm that Intel-optimized sklearn is being used through the message obtained as a result of execution of the below piece of code.

```
from sklearnex import patch_sklearn, unpatch_sklearn
patch_sklearn() # this will set parameters such that the stock version of sklearn will be called
from sklearn import datasets, svm, metrics, preprocessing
from sklearn.linear_model import LinearRegression
from sklearn.model_selection import train_test_split

Intel(R) Extension for Scikit-learn* enabled (https://github.com/intel/scikit-learn-intelex)
```

- *Step 3:* Subsequently, the flattening must be carried out. Followed by that, the training dataset and the test dataset split must be carried out. It is totally up to the developer to decide the split percentage. It is important to normalize the input values and the same is presented in the below code snippet.

```
# digits.data stores flattened ndarray
digits = datasets.load_diabetes()
X,Y = digits.data, digits.target

# Split dataset into 80% train and 20% test
X_train, X_test, Y_train, Y_test = train_test_split(X, Y, test_size=0.2, shuffle=True)

# normalize the input values by scaling each feature by its maximum absolute value
X_train = preprocessing.maxabs_scale(X_train)
X_test = preprocessing.maxabs_scale(X_test)
```

- *Step 4:* The linear regressor has to be created next. Once the model is all ready, it is important to save the model in a file.

```
# Create a linear regressor
model = LinearRegression()

# learn the digits on the train subset
fit_st = time.time()
model.fit(X_train, Y_train)
fit_time = fit_st-time.time()

# Save the model to a file
filename = 'finalized_svm_model_unpatch.sav'
joblib.dump(model, filename)
```

- *Step 5:* Well, it is now time to run the model. One can see the running time needed for the model printed on the execution.

```
loaded_model = joblib.load(filename)
t1 = time.time()
Y_pred = loaded_model.predict(X_test)
Intel_optimized_RandomForest_time= time.time()-t1
print(time.time()-t1)
0.0012395381927490234
```

6.5 Classification – A Must-Know Concept

The first question that normally arises is: What is the difference between regression and classification? We shall let the reader understand this point first.

Well, to start with, regression and classification both come under supervised learning algorithms! (Yes, supervised, labeled). Both these have extensive usage in machine learning and both use the labeled dataset. Then, where do they differ? The problems that they solve are different and that defines their difference.

As discussed, regression predicts continuous variables, such as salary, marks, age etc. Classification classify variables like male/female, pass/fail, false/true, spam/legitimate etc. (It classifies, that's it.) Classification divides the given dataset into classes based on the parameters considered. An example will be very helpful.

Gmail is the best example. Gmail classifies email as legitimate or spam. The model is trained with millions of emails and takes many parameters into consideration. Whenever a new email pops up, the classification shall be done as "Inbox, Spam, Promotions or updates." If spam, it goes to spam box. If legitimate, it goes to Inbox.

There are many famous and frequently used classification algorithms:

- Support Vector Machines (SVM)
- K-Nearest Neighbors
- Kernel SVM
- Logistic Regression
- Naïve Bayes
- Decision Tree Classification
- Random Forest Classification

It is good to understand and learn all of these. But it would be beyond the scope of this book. So, we select K-Nearest Neighbors (KNN) and Support Vector Machines (SVM) for further discussion.

6.5.1 K-Nearest Neighbor (KNN)

KNN is one of the easiest and most frequently used approaches, like SVM. KNN is also based on supervised learning algorithms. It is based on a very simple approach. Based on history, the current case is predicted, i.e., when the new data are sent in for classification, based on the similarity of data available in the past, the new one gets classified, i.e., the most similar category will be found and the new data entry shall be classified into that.

Simply speaking, new data can be classified with ease into the most similar category with KNN in place.

The next question would be, where can we use KNN? It has been used for classification and regression. But, like SVM, KNN works better when used with classification and hence is used preferentially for classification.

KNN has two very important characteristics:

1. It is referred as non-parametric.
2. It is also said to be lazy learner algorithm.

It is important to understand what non-parametric means. It means the algorithm does not make any assumptions on the characteristics underlying the data.

Next, what is lazy learning? Nothing happens immediately in this approach. "Lazy learner" means that the algorithm does not learn anything from the training dataset at that instance. But it stores the entire dataset during the classification and then does the action on the dataset. It infers that there is no specialized training phase and uses all the data for training while classification is underway.

As ever, an example would be useful. If someone wants to classify a fruit, such as an orange, when the input is sent in, the algorithm works with the similarity concept. Based on the similarly of the features, it would then classify the fruit as an orange or not.

In the KNN, remember, K is the king. Data scientists have preferred K to be an odd number when the classes are even. K could be 1, 3, 5 or 7 when there are two classes. One should also note that, when K = 1, it is the nearest neighbor algorithm.

It is now time to approach KNN step by step:

- Can we select the number K of the neighbors? Yes, it is the first step.
- One should calculate the Euclidean distance of the number K of the neighbors

Then, take the K nearest neighbors as per the calculated Euclidean distance.

- Start counting. Among these K neighbors, count the number of data points in each category.
- Assign the new data points to the category for which the number of the neighbors is highest.
- The model is ready.

An example will be very handy and make it easier to understand. One can have a look at Figure 6.18.

The problem statement is presented pictorially in Figure 6.19, where the new data entry has to be classified as a red star or a green triangle.

Case 1 – When K is Chosen to be 1
If K is chosen as 1, then the task becomes easier, and this is the simplest option. The input data get classified as Class A. One can easily understand this from Figure 6.20.

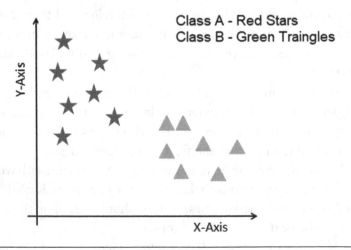

Figure 6.18   The assumed scenario.

Figure 6.19   The assumed scenario – with a new entrant.

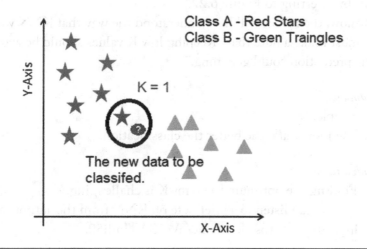

Figure 6.20   Case 1: K = 1.

Case 2 – When K is Chosen to be 3

Let us calculate the Euclidean distance between the data points when K is chosen as 3. The Euclidean distance is the distance between two points (can be done through other methods also; Python has in-built functions to help the programmers). One could have a look at Figure 6.21 to understand how KNN works when the K value is chosen to be 3.

- Class A = 1 count
- Class B =2 count.
- So, naturally, the new entry is classified as B. (I.e. green triangles)

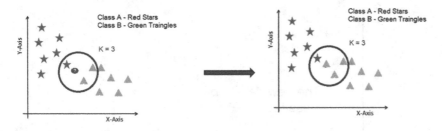

Figure 6.21   Case 2: K = 3.

Case 3 – When K is Chosen to be 7

Here is the scenario when K is set as 7. One can understand how this works by referring to Figure 6.22.

By now, the reader will have understood the way that KNN works. One must make a note that "Keeping low K values should be avoided as the prediction could go wrong."

Advantages

- Simple.
- The more data, the better the classification.

Disadvantage

- Finding the optimum value for K is challenging.

    One can listen to a brief note on KNN from the authors by listening to https://youtu.be/nVgZbVUmh50.

- Class A = 4 count
- Class B =3 count.
- So, naturally, the new entry is classified as A. (I.e. Red Stars)

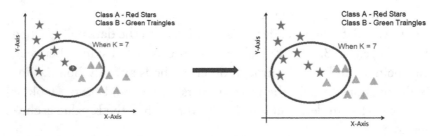

Figure 6.22   Case 2: K = 7.

6.5.2 Implementation of KNN

It is time to implement the KNN with the oneAPI. The reader will be presented with a step-by-step explanation for implementation and results shall be discussed at the end.

- *Step 1:* It is important to do the necessary imports. The code is made available in https://github.com/shriramkv/Machine LearningwithoneAPI for quick reference.

```
#importing necessary libraries
from sklearn.preprocessing import OneHotEncoder
from sklearn import datasets
import sklearn.model_selection as model_selection
from sklearn.metrics import accuracy_score
from sklearn.metrics import f1_score
import pandas as pd
import time
import numpy as np
import numpy.ma as ma
```

- *Step 2:* We load the connect-4 game dataset. We predict the win/loss/draw outcome for one of the players based on the moves played in the given dataset. We perform multiple preprocessing steps and apply onehot encoding.

```
connect4 = pd.read_csv('connect-4.data')
data = connect4.iloc[:,:42].replace(['x', 'o', 'b'], [0,1,2])

keep = .25
subsetLen = int(keep*data.shape[0])

X = np.byte( data.iloc[:subsetLen,:].to_numpy() )
#np.random.seed(42)
#np.random.shuffle(X)
X = X[:subsetLen,:42]
enc = OneHotEncoder(handle_unknown='ignore')
enc.fit(X)
enc.categories_

XOHE = np.short(enc.transform(X).toarray() )# X one hot encoded
Data_y = connect4.iloc[:,42].to_numpy()
#np.random.shuffle(Data_y)
y =  Data_y[:subsetLen]
X_train, X_test, y_train, y_test = model_selection.train_test_split(XOHE, y, train_size=0.80,
                                    test_size=0.20, random_state=101)
```

- *Step 3:* We are going to compare the performance of the stock sklearn and the Intel-optimized sklearn for the KNN implementation. Hence, the patch and unpatch approach is followed as shown below in the code.

```
# In[22]:
y.shape

# In[21]:
from sklearnex import patch_sklearn, unpatch_sklearn
unpatch_sklearn()
from sklearn.metrics import classification_report

def predict( linear ):
    import numpy as np
    time_patch_predict = time.time()
    y_pred = linear.predict(X_test)
    elapsed = time.time() - time_patch_predict
    return elapsed, y_pred

def fit():
    start = time.time()
    linear = KNeighborsClassifier(n_neighbors=7).fit(X_train, y_train)
    time_patch_fit = time.time() - start
    return time_patch_fit, linear
```

- *Step 4:* The Intel-optimized sklearn comes into the picture below. The reports are generated which can be used as the metrics by which to compare the stock sklearn and the Intel-optimized sklearn. One can see clearly that KNN is brought into the picture.

```
from sklearn.metrics import classification_report
patch_sklearn()
from sklearn.neighbors import KNeighborsClassifier
time_fit, linear = fit()
time_predict, y_pred = predict(linear)
target_names = ['win', 'loss', 'draw']
print("file as is ")
print(classification_report(y_test, y_pred, target_names=target_names))
print('Elapsed time: {:.2f} sec'.format( time_fit + time_predict))
```

- *Step: 5:* The piece of code below should help in understanding the performance metrics with the stock sklearn.

```
from sklearnex import patch_sklearn, unpatch_sklearn
from sklearn.metrics import classification_report
unpatch_sklearn()
from sklearn.neighbors import KNeighborsClassifier
time_fit, linear = fit()
time_predict, y_pred = predict(linear)
target_names = ['win', 'loss', 'draw']
print("explicit unpatch ")
print(classification_report(y_test, y_pred, target_names=target_names))
print('Elapsed time: {:.2f} sec'.format( time_fit + time_predict))
```

One can see that the Intel extension of the scikit-learn is clearly enabled and is visible through a message which is received during the execution. The elapsed time is also presented along with the precision, recall, F1 score, etc., all of which can be compared against the stock scikit-learn results.

```
Intel(R) Extension for Scikit-learn* enabled (https://github.com/intel/scikit-learn-intelex)
file as is
              precision    recall  f1-score   support

        win       0.44      0.13      0.20       231
       loss       0.72      0.53      0.61       614
       draw       0.85      0.96      0.90      2533

   accuracy                           0.83      3378
  macro avg       0.67      0.54      0.57      3378
weighted avg      0.80      0.83      0.80      3378

Elapsed time: 0.06 sec
```

The below screenshot presents the results for the stock version of scikit-learn. One can see that the elapsed time is much higher, 0.78 seconds, than the 0.06 seconds mark that we arrived at with the Intel-optimized scikit-learn.

```
  explicit unpatch
              precision    recall  f1-score   support

        win       0.38      0.13      0.19       231
       loss       0.75      0.56      0.64       614
       draw       0.86      0.96      0.91      2533

   accuracy                           0.83      3378
  macro avg       0.66      0.55      0.58      3378
weighted avg      0.81      0.83      0.81      3378

  Elapsed time: 0.78 sec
```

The percentage improvement in terms of the execution time one could achieve while using Intel-optimized scikit-learn is presented below, with 233% improvement as observed in the screenshot below, a result which is definitely appreciated by developers.

```
100*(1-0.3)/0.3

233.33333333333334
```

6.6 Loss and Cost Function, Bias and Variance Trade-off, Regularization, Feature Selection and Hyperparameter Tuning

Linear regression tries to predict the target variable, minimizing the error over the independent input variables. This helps to understand the model accuracy with respect to the accurate predictions done on the test inputs, which are unseen. Regularization is the method used to prevent overfitting of the model generated. Let's understand a bit more about the underfitting and overfitting of a model, with a suitable example. To understand them in a detailed manner, it is mandatory to touch upon certain terminologies, like loss and cost functions.

As linear regression is a supervised machine learning model which focuses on reducing the errors, it is important to understand the loss function, cost function and gradient descent at a bare minimum.

Loss function is the simplest way to understand how well the given linear regression machine learning model fits the specific training dataset. This basically calculates the prediction error. Say if we consider a ground truth for the values and if there is a major difference between the predicted and ground truth values, then we could say that the loss function is high. Loss functions are commonly used for hyperparameter tuning or optimization.

Cost Function is the collective loss function across all observations in the training dataset. In terms of a linear regression, an example of a loss function could be the least squared error and the cost function is the mean squared error (MSE).

So, let's understand what exactly an "error" in machine learning is. Consider Figure 6.23 below. This depicts the error, in fact, the training and validation error in terms of Bias and Variance.

Error is simply a measure of how well the machine learning algorithm will make predictions for the unseen dataset. Mainly, the errors are divided into reducible and irreducible errors, as shown in Figure 6.24.

Bias and Variance are basically the reducible errors in machine learning. What do we mean by that? This simply means that there is a chance that you can reduce these errors and improve the accuracy of

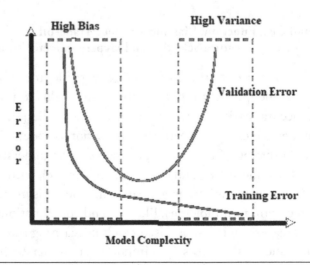

Figure 6.23 Error and model complexity.

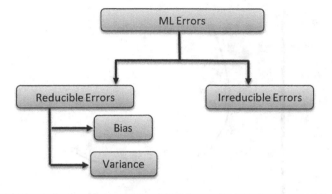

Figure 6.24 Errors in machine learning.

the model. On the contrary, irreducible errors are those present in the model by default.

What is bias? Bias is the difference in prediction values and actual values expected to be predicted by the model. This shows the model's incapability of understanding the correlation between the various data points. Bias can be of two types: low bias and high bias.

Low bias is where the model includes fewer assumptions about the target function. Say, for example, an algorithm like a linear regression algorithm is simple and learns fast, and will have a higher bias. That means a model with a higher bias would not match the training dataset. In other words, a model will underfit if there is a high bias and the model will overfit if there is a low bias.

Consider the example where we need to predict the salary of a person based on their educational qualification. Consider we did an experiential analysis of asking 100 people in person, and if we consider the data taken for plotting the salary and age, it is an easy task. The model might not bring accurate results because of underfitting or high bias.

Say, for example, if we consider many independent variables like age, sex, level of education, profession, etc., even though the model becomes complex and tries to generalize to make a good prediction on the training dataset, it fails to bring in good predictions on the test dataset. This is nothing but overfitting or high variance as shown in Figure 6.25.

In terms of linear regression, we can have various independent variables, like age, level of education, sex, profession, etc., as mentioned

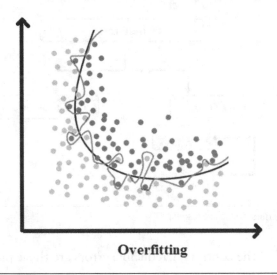

Overfitting

Figure 6.25 Overfitting of data points.

earlier. All of these independent variables may take up different values (or weights) to predict the salary in various permutations and combinations. This is where the hyperparameter optimization or tuning or weights for hyperparameters come into the picture. These adjustments of weights carried out on the independent variables is called regularization and is done to make the best prediction on the test dataset by the model.

So, what exactly is *Regularization*?

By regularization, you are making the model select the best features that will help the model predict the best in a test dataset. In simple terms, we could say, regularization helps in feature selection of the model. To keep it in terms of bias and variance, regularization helps to find a trade-off between high bias and high variance, as shown in Figure 6.26. This is nothing but the bias–variance trade-off scenario in a machine learning problem. That means that we would like to reduce the accuracy on the training dataset from, say, 100 % to 80 %, but still achieve an accuracy of say 50 to 80 % on the test or unseen dataset.

Even though this is somewhat beyond the scope of this book, it is good to understand that there are a few major types of regularization in linear regression. They are lasso regression, which uses the L1 regularization technique, ridge regression which uses the L2

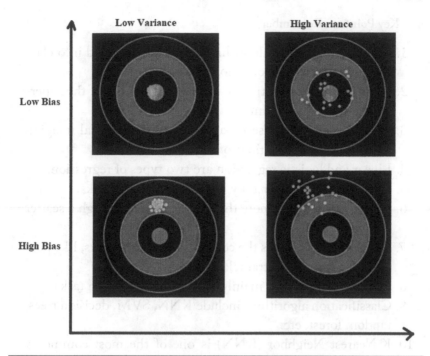

Figure 6.26 Bias and variance trade-off.

regularization technique and elastic net regression, which uses a combination of both ridge and lasso to train the model.

We hope this has given the reader a quick understanding about the errors in machine learning and how to reduce the errors in linear regression to obtain greater model accuracy.

Well, we hope the reader has a good time going through this chapter. It's time to explore the SVM classification algorithm which awaits you in the next chapter, Chapter 7.

Resources

- Vasudevan, S.K., Pulari, S.R., & Vasudevan, S. (2021). Deep Learning: A Comprehensive Guide (1st ed.). Chapman and Hall/CRC Press. https://doi.org/10.1201/9781003185635
- Murphy, Kevin P., & Bach, F. 2012). Machine Learning: A Probabilistic Perspective. Cambridge, MA, MIT Press.
- https://www.youtube.com/playlist?list=PL3uLubnzL2Tl -7fugIeCk4-l4HVVdn5_v
- https://dionysus.psych.wisc.edu/iaml_2020/unit-06.html

6.7 Key Points to Remember

1. Supervised learning algorithms are mainly divided into classification and regression algorithms.
2. Spam email classification is an example of a use of the supervised learning algorithm.
3. Trend analysis, time series analysis and biomedical imaging are all various applications of regression analysis.
4. Linear and logistic regression are two types of regression.
5. Linear regression is mainly used for regression tasks.
6. Linear regression is more than fitting a line through a scatter of data points.
7. Linear regression uses the correlation of data points, like positive, negative or neutral relationships.
8. Logistic regression is mainly used for classification tasks.
9. Classification algorithms include KNN, SVM, decision trees, random forest, etc.
10. K-Nearest Neighbor (KNN) is one of the most commonly used classification algorithms.
11. KNN has two very important aspects: it is non-parametric and a lazy learner algorithm.
12. K is the number of neighbors in a KNN algorithm.
13. The more data, the better the KNN classification.
14. Loss and cost function, bias and variance trade-off, regularization, feature selection and hyperparameter tuning are important in linear regression.
15. Lasso, ridge and elastic net regression are the common regularization techniques used in regression problems.

Quiz Questions (Answer it Yourself, Folks)

1. What is supervised learning?
2. Can we classify spam email classification with a supervised learning algorithm?
3. List the types of regression algorithms.
4. What is linear regression and explain the algorithm step-by-steps.

5. What is classification and list the various classification algorithms.
6. What is KNN? Can you explain KNN with an example?
7. What are the two major aspects of KNN algorithms?
8. Can you explain what "K" stands for in "KNN"?
9. What is the major difference between logistic regression and linear regression?
10. What is a lazy learner algorithm?
11. Differentiate between a loss function and a cost function.
12. What is regularization?
13. What is the bias–variance trade-off?
14. What is overfitting?
15. What is hyperparameter tuning?

7

SUPPORT VECTOR MACHINES (SVM)

An Exploration

Learning Objectives

After going through this chapter, the reader should be able to understand the following:

- What is SVM?
- How does it work?
- Implementation and testing
- Costs and functions of SVM

7.1 SVM – Support Vector Machines

To start with, SVM is very easy to use, as well as to learn. Data scientists claim that SVM offers greater accuracy than other classifiers we work with. SVM is mostly used in e-mail classification, handwriting recognition, etc. The reader will be introduced to SVM and have it explained clearly in this section.

SVM is usable for both regression and classification problems, but, most commonly, it is used for classification problems rather than regression ones. The main aim of SVM is all about creating an optimum line or a decision boundary. The decision boundary will enable segregation of the dataset into classes. Also, it will enable the correct classification of new data in the future.

The appropriate decision boundary is referred to technically as a hyperplane. It is very important for the reader to understand the terminologies used in SVM. They are presented one after another in this chapter in a detailed manner.

DOI: 10.1201/9781003393122-7

7.1.1 Hyperplane

This is an important term. It is a plane which separates (i.e., enables grouping of) objects that belong to different classes. This line helps in classifying the data points (i.e., the red stars and green triangles). One can refer to Figure 7.1 to understand the hyperplane concept.

The dimension of a hyperplane is a variable too. Is it possible that way? Yes, it is. One should refer to Figure 7.1. It has two features and hence one straight line is sufficient. If there are three features, yes, it must be a two-dimensional plane.

7.1.2 Support Vectors

One should refer again to Figure 7.1. The red stars and the green triangles are the support vectors. These points are very close to the hyperplane. These data points are the ones that would affect the position of the hyperplane as well. These points are vectors. Since they have a role in deciding the hyperplane's placement, they are called support vectors.

7.1.3 Margin

This is a gap. If the margin between two classes is larger, then it is a good margin. Otherwise, it is considered to be bad. In simple terms, a margin is a gap between two lines on closely located class points.

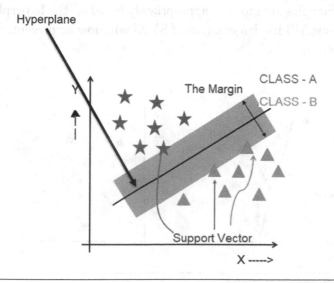

Figure 7.1   The SVM – a complete picture.

By referring again to Figure 7.1, one can understand that the margin can be calculated as the perpendicular distance from the line to the support vectors (red stars and green triangles)

7.1.4 How Does SVM Work?

Simple! One should group/segregate the dataset (i.e., non-classified to classified) in the best possible way.

The readers know what a margin is all about. A margin is a gap between two lines on closely located class points. Now, the task in hand is simple. One must select/draw a hyperplane with a maximum margin between the support vectors from the input dataset. The greater the margin, the larger the gap.

The reader will be taken through the process step by step:

One should first generate hyperplanes. Three such planes are generated, brown followed by blue and red, as shown in Figure 7.2. As anyone can see, brown and blue have failed miserably to classify the dataset. This reflects a high error rate. So, red is very appropriate, and it does the classification properly. So, what do we do? The answer is obvious: choose the best line. The best-drawn line (the "line-of-best-fit") is presented as a black line on the right-hand side of Figure 7.2.

That is it. One could now understand that all the red stars and green triangles are grouped appropriately based on the hyperplane.

The oneAPI implementation of SVM will now be presented in the next section.

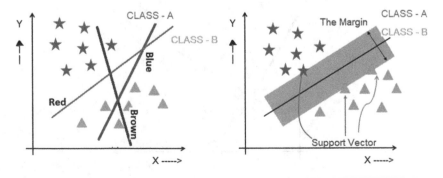

Figure 7.2 Hyperplane selection.

7.2 SVM Implementation

It is time to implement the SVM, using the oneAPI open programming model. The reader will be presented with a step-by-step explanation of the implementation, with the results discussed at the end.

- *Step 1:* It is important to carry out the necessary imports. The code is made available in the link https://github.com/shri-ramkv/MachineLearningwithoneAPI for quicker reference.

```python
#importing necessary libraries
from sklearn.preprocessing import OneHotEncoder
from sklearn import datasets
import sklearn.model_selection as model_selection
from sklearn.metrics import accuracy_score
from sklearn.metrics import f1_score
import pandas as pd
import time
import numpy as np
import numpy.ma as ma
```

- *Step 2:* We load the Connect-4 game dataset. We predict the win/loss/draw outcome of one of the players based on the moves played in the given dataset and perform multiple pre-processing steps and apply onehot encoding.

```python
connect4 = pd.read_csv('connect-4.data')
#applying transformations to data
data = connect4.iloc[:,:42].replace(['x', 'o', 'b'], [0,1,2])
keep = .25
subsetLen = int(keep*data.shape[0])
X = np.byte( data.iloc[:subsetLen,:].to_numpy() )
enc = OneHotEncoder(handle_unknown='ignore')
enc.fit(X)
enc.categories_

XOHE = np.short(enc.transform(X).toarray() )# X one hot encoded

Data_y = connect4.iloc[:,42].to_numpy()
#np.random.shuffle(Data_y)
y = Data_y[:subsetLen]
```

```python
X_train, X_test, y_train, y_test = model_selection.train_test_split(XOHE, y, train_size=0.80, test_size=0.20,
y.shape
```

- *Step 3:* We are going to compare the performance of the stock sklearn and Intel optimized sklearn for the SVM implementation. Hence, the patch and unpatch approach is followed as shown below in the code.

```
from sklearnex import patch_sklearn, unpatch_sklearn
unpatch_sklearn()
from sklearn.metrics import classification_report

def predict( linear ):
    import numpy as np
    time_patch_predict = time.time()
    y_pred = linear.predict(X_test)
    elapsed = time.time() - time_patch_predict
    return elapsed, y_pred
# applying fit to the svm model
def fit():
    start = time.time()
    linear = svm.SVC(kernel='linear', C=100).fit(X_train, y_train)
    time_patch_fit = time.time() - start
    return time_patch_fit, linear
```

- *Step 4:* The Intel optimized sklearn comes into the picture as seen below. The reports are generated which can be used as the metrics by which to compare the stock sklearn and Intel optimized sklearn.

```
# using intel optimized sklearn
from sklearn.metrics import classification_report
patch_sklearn()
from sklearn import svm
time_fit, linear = fit()
time_predict, y_pred = predict(linear)
target_names = ['win', 'loss', 'draw']
#generating reports
print("file as is ")
print(classification_report(y_test, y_pred, target_names=target_names))
print('Elapsed time: {:.2f} sec'.format( time_fit + time_predict))
```

- *Step 5:* The below piece of code will help the reader to understand the performance metrics with the stock sklearn.

```
# Using stock sklearn
from sklearnex import patch_sklearn, unpatch_sklearn
from sklearn.metrics import classification_report
unpatch_sklearn("svc")
from sklearn import svm
time_fit, linear = fit()
time_predict, y_pred = predict(linear)
target_names = ['win', 'loss', 'draw']
#generating reports
print("explicit unpatch ")
print(classification_report(y_test, y_pred, target_names=target_names))
print('Elapsed time: {:.2f} sec'.format( time_fit + time_predict))
```

One can see that the Intel extension of the scikit-learn is clearly enabled and is visible through a message which we received during the execution. The elapsed time is also presented along with the precision, recall, F1 score, etc., which can be compared against the stock scikit-learn results.

```
Intel(R) Extension for Scikit-learn* enabled (https://github.com/intel/scikit-learn-intelex)
file as is
                precision    recall  f1-score   support

         win      0.45       0.02      0.04       231
        loss      0.68       0.59      0.63       614
        draw      0.85       0.95      0.89       2533

    accuracy                           0.82       3378
   macro avg      0.66       0.52      0.52       3378
weighted avg      0.79       0.82      0.79       3378

Elapsed time: 11.14 sec
```

The below screenshot presents the results for the stock version of scikit-learn. One can see that the elapsed time is so high, 75 seconds more than the 11 seconds mark that we arrived at with the Intel optimized scikit-learn.

```
explicit unpatch
                precision    recall  f1-score   support

         win      0.45       0.02      0.04       231
        loss      0.68       0.59      0.63       614
        draw      0.85       0.95      0.89       2533

    accuracy                           0.82       3378
   macro avg      0.66       0.52      0.52       3378
weighted avg      0.79       0.82      0.79       3378

Elapsed time: 75.02 sec
```

The percentage improvement one could arrive at when using the Intel optimized scikit-learn in terms of the execution time is presented below. An improvement of 543% is achieved, matching the type of effect which software developers require.

```
100*(74.13 - 11.52) / 11.52
543.4895833333334
```

7.3 Key Points to Remember

- Regression and classification both come under the heading of unsupervised learning algorithms.
- Data scientists claim that SVM offers greater accuracy than other classifiers we work with.
- SVM is mostly used in e-mail classification, handwriting recognition, etc.
- The main aim of the SVM is all about creating an optimum line or a decision boundary.
- A hyperplane is a plane that separates (i.e., enables grouping of) objects that belong to different classes.

Quiz

1. Under which situations can SVM be used? Specify several types of applications where SVM could be the best fit.
2. How important are hyperplanes? Explain your answer.
3. What is a support vector? What is the influence of the support vector? Clarify these answers.

8

DECISION TREES

Learning Objectives

After reading this chapter, the reader should be able to understand the following:

- What is the purpose and function of decision trees?
- Classification problem with decision trees.
- Random forest classifer.
- Advantages of decision trees and random forest.
- Applications of decision trees and random forest.
- Random forest or decision trees?
- Implementation

8.1 Introduction

Classification is a supervised learning method which mainly consists of two steps, namely model construction and model usage. In the model construction, given a dataset with a set of attributes where one is a target attribute (a class label), we need to split the dataset into a training dataset and a test dataset. We need to use a training set to build a model for a target attribute as a function of other attributes. In the model usage step, the test dataset was used for prediction purposes to check how the model built assigns a target attribute (numerical or categorical) to unseen examples (accuracy of prediction). The known target attribute from the test dataset is compared with the result from the model. Accuracy is calculated as the percentage of the test dataset correctly classified by the model. Recalling all these and, upon considering the golf dataset as an example where various weather-related attributes are provided, we need to predict whether we will be able to play golf on a particular day.

The various independent parameters, like outlook, temperature, humidity and wind, are given in the golf dataset. The target variable is play. This is to predict whether we can play or not given the values of the independent variables as shown in Figure 8.1.

DOI: 10.1201/9781003393122-8

Training Set:

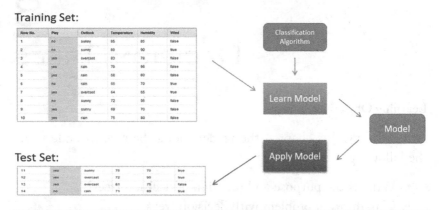

Test Set:

Figure 8.1 Recap of classification.

In this chapter, we will develop an understanding of the classification algorithms decision trees and random forest, and we will walk you through a detailed implementation of random forest as these algorithms are very commonly used for many real-time applications. So let's get started.

8.2 What Do Decision Trees Involve?

Consider the following diagram in Figure 8.2.

In this example, a person decides about his current action plan. He assesses himself by checking with the conditional statements using if–else as shown in Figure 8.3.

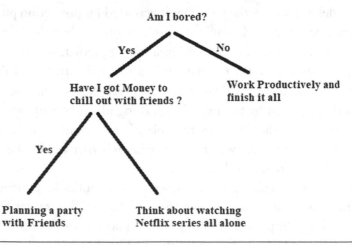

Figure 8.2 A simple decision tree model.

Check if (bored) ☹

    Check if he has money☺

        If so plan a party with friends ☺

    Else:

        Think about watching a Netflix series ☹

Else:

    Work productively and finish it all ☺

Figure 8.3 Conditional explanation of decision trees using if – else.

Hence, by now, it should be clear to you what a decision tree is all about! Decision trees are flowchart-like tree structures, which use a conditional control statement to decide the path they has to take to provide favorable results or possible consequences. They are considered to be among the best algorithms for supervised learning problems. In order to go a little deeper into the tree structure of a decision tree, the nodes are the attributes, the branches are the outcomes for the attributes (say, yes or no) which help to decide the path and the path from a leaf to the root are the classification rules, with one leaf being one of the possible consequences.

In the example shown in Figure 8.4, it shows that the root node "Am I bored" is also a decision node that helps to make decisions

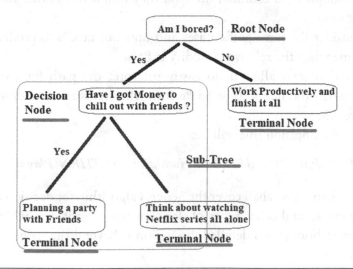

Figure 8.4 Explanation of nodes in a decision tree.

like which path needs to be followed. Also, in the same figure, you can see the terminal nodes or the leaf nodes, which are the probable consequences. They are shown in green boxes as a sub-tree or branch for a better understanding.

There are two main types of decision trees:

1. *Decision trees for categorical variables (classification)*: This type of decision tree gives you a Yes/No or True/False prediction.
2. *Decision trees for continuous variables (regression)*: This type of decision tree helps you to predict the income (unknown) of an employee in a company, considering some attribute values like occupation, age, etc.

8.3 Classification Problem with Decision Trees

Decision trees help to choose the optimal path from the leaf nodes. For this, the metric used is known as "purity." Don't worry, it is simple. If the node is pure, it will have all its data belonging to one class. Classification is crystal clear.

Let's consider an example of the golf dataset shown in Figure 8.5. Given the classification rule,

IF Outlook = 'rain' AND Wind = 'false' THEN Play = 'yes';

This example is so common that you may find it from other internet sources too.

Consider the same golf dataset and now our task is to predict the outcome when the relative humidity is 85%.

Decision trees allow us to easily interpret the path for the outcome when the humidity is 85 % from the tree structure shown in Figure 8.5.

The classification rule will be:

IF Outlook = 'Humidity' and Humidity > 85 THEN Play = 'no'

In this chapter, we shall cover the general algorithm for decision trees. There are several other types of decision tree algorithms, which we will cover briefly, as a detailed discussion is beyond the scope of this book.

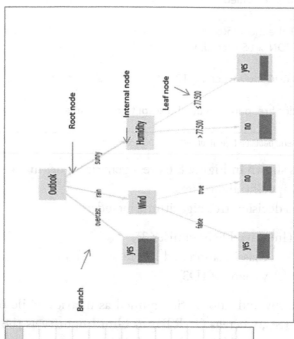

Row No.	Play	Outlook	Temperature	Humidity	Wind
1	no	sunny	85	85	false
2	no	sunny	80	90	true
3	yes	overcast	83	78	false
4	yes	rain	70	95	false
5	yes	rain	68	80	false
6	no	rain	65	70	true
7	yes	overcast	64	65	true
8	no	sunny	72	95	false
9	yes	sunny	69	70	false
10	yes	rain	75	80	false
11	yes	sunny	75	70	true
12	yes	overcast	72	90	true
13	yes	overcast	81	75	false
14	no	rain	71	80	true

Figure 8.5 Application of classification rules for finding an optimal solution.

Given a training set S, construct a tree T
   IF all examples in set S belong to some class C OR set S is sufficiently 'pure',
   THEN make a leaf labeled C
   ELSE
       SELECT the most informative attribute A;
       PARTITION set S according to values of A;
   REPEAT
       CONSTRUCT sub-trees T1, T2,... for the subsets of S;
   UNTIL
       All nodes are 'pure' OR attribute split not possible;

Figure 8.6   Generic decision tree algorithm.

The details shown in Figure 8.6 are a generic algorithm and might vary between specific algorithms.

The various decision tree algorithms include:

1. ID3 → (Iterative Dichotomiser 3)
2. CART → (Classification and Regression Tree)
3. C4.5 → (A variant of ID3)

ID3 uses entropy and information gained as metrics while building the decision trees, whereas CART uses Gini Impurity as the metric. C4.5 is an extension of ID3 and uses the Gain ratio as the metric.

8.3.1 Challenges in Decision Trees

When building an optimal tree, we want the tree to be as short as possible.

- Which attribute to select first to achieve that?
  and
  Which attribute to select next?
- Where to perform Attribute to split the tree?

The idea is to select for the root node; the attribute which brings the most information will be the best predictor. The same analogy is to be used when deciding on the next node.

In order to perform selection for the best attribute, there are certain metrics used in decision trees.

You should know the appropriate terminology if you want to dive deep into the concepts. The way to pick the starting test condition in Decision Trees could be decided by these metrics. Let's get started.

Impurity/Entropy is the measure of randomness or disorder or simply it is the uncertainty present in the data. This is an attribute selection measure. We can calculate entropy by the following equation:

$$E(S) = \sum_{i=1}^{c} -p_i \, log_2 \, p_i$$

where S is the set of all instances in the dataset,

   c is the number of classes,

   p_i is the event probability.

A simple example could be, say, if we flip a coin, there is a 50 % uncertainty that we may always get heads or tails; this uncertainty is always there for each flip, which is considered the entropy. The representation of low and high entropy is presented in Figure 8.7.

Information gain can be defined as the amount of information gained about a random variable or signal from observing another random variable. You may calculate the information gain as follows:

   If S is the total collection of data,

Information Gain

   = *Entropy* (S) − [*weighted average* * *Entropy* (*each feature*)]

To make it simpler to understand,

     Information Gain(*Parent, Child*) = *E*(*Parent*) − *E*(*Child*)

Gini Impurity is a method for splitting the nodes when the target variable is categorical.

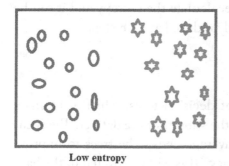
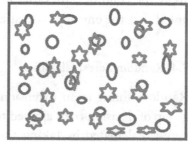

Low entropy   High Entropy

Figure 8.7   Representations of low and high entropy.

$$Gini\ Impurity = 1 - Gini$$

For this, we need to know how to calculate Gini:

Gini is the probability of correctly labeling a randomly chosen element if it is randomly labeled according to the distribution of labels in the node.

$$Gini = \sum_{i=1}^{c} p_i^2$$

Mathematically,

$$Gini\ Impurity = 1 - \sum_{i=1}^{c} p_i^2$$

All these help the decision tree algorithms to be suitable for attribute selection in various algorithms like ID3, CART, etc. All these metrics help decision trees in various algorithms to decide which attribute will give the most appropriate path to reach the optimal solution.

It is time for us to see a generic example of a decision tree to understand how we make use of the conditions given and how we try to reduce the entropy to reach the optimal solution. Consider we are given an animal dataset with varied height, weight and color. We are given certain conditions to consider, like color = yellow, height≥10, etc. Let's see how we find a tree using the decision tree method to reduce the entropy at each step.

As shown in Figures 8.8 and 8.9, given a dataset of various animals with varied attributes and conditions, entropy is calculated and various conditions are then applied based on the gain. Next, we need to apply the conditions in order to recalculate the entropy and it can be noted that the entropy is drastically reduced at each step.

8.4 Random Forest Classifier

Random forest is an extension of decision trees, which contains a group of decision trees applied to the subsets of the dataset. The accuracy is calculated by taking the average across the trees to improve the predictions with greater accuracy. This will be covered in the bagging model in ensemble modeling, where we learn to use multiple

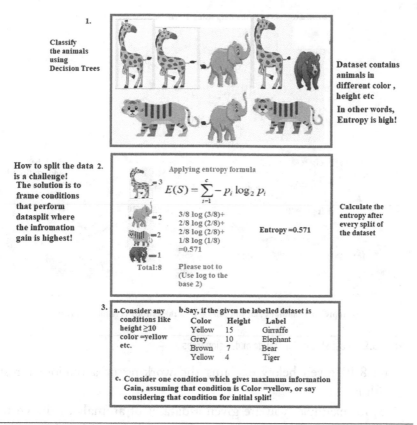

Figure 8.8 Steps in excision tree illustration.

classifiers to find the optimal solution for the problem with better performance. We will touch upon random forest in the next chapter also.

Steps for random forest are as follows:

1. Given the dataset or training dataset, select random samples.
2. Construct a decision tree for each of the samples.
3. Use the ensemble method to perform majority voting.
4. Finally, the optimal prediction will be based on the most voted result.

Bagging is an ensemble model which is also called a bootstrap aggregation. Random forest uses bagging where bootstrapping is the initial step, where the dataset or training samples are provided as random samples. After this process, they aggregate the results to find the optimal solution, which is why bagging is also called bootstrap aggregation. A detailed explanation of bagging will be presented in Chapter 9.

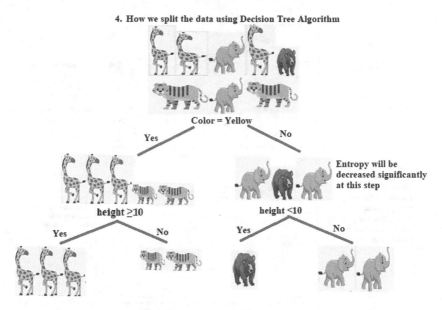

4. How we split the data using Decision Tree Algorithm

Color = Yellow

Yes

No

Entropy will be decreased significantly at this step

height ≥10

height <10

Yes

No

Yes

No

This is how we apply the conditions and you can see how the entropy is reduced at each step.

Figure 8.9 Last step in illustration of decision trees.

Figure 8.10 given below explains the working of a random forest algorithm.

Say, for example, you are given a dataset of animals as shown in Figure 8.11, and your job is to classify animals correctly using a random forest algorithm. The random forest algorithm uses its dataset and creates random samples from the given animal dataset. It is fed to the various decision tree models. Here, each of the decision trees creates its predictions by using the different conditions given. For example, decision tree 1 uses color = yellow as the initial condition and proceeds to build the tree using the entropy and information gain. Maybe decision tree 2 finds the information gain is more for the condition height ≥20 and proceeds building the tree, etc. Thus, each of the decision tree models might use different conditions for initial attribute selection. Once the decision trees are formed, then comes the ensemble part, using majority voting. Say in our example, given in Figure 8.11, two of the decision trees have predicted class 1, which is toucan (a brightly colored bird with large curved beak) and one of the decision trees has predicted class 2, which is the Gouldian finch (a small bird available in a variety of striking, vibrant colors). According

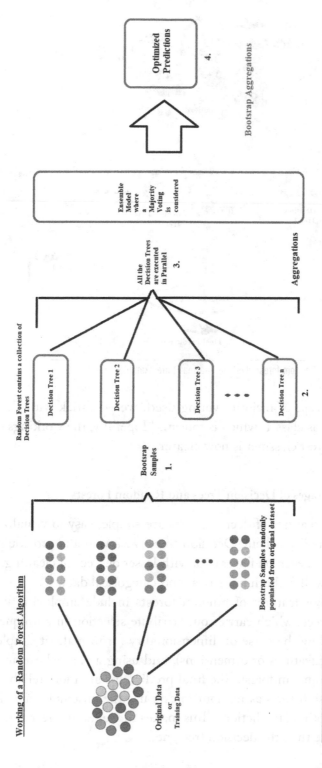

Figure 8.10 Operation of a random forest algorithm.

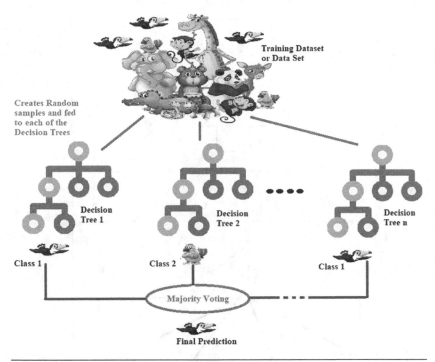

Figure 8.11   Random forest classifier – a real-time example.

to the concept of majority voting used, we will stick with the final prediction as class 1, which is toucan. Hopefully, the workings of the random forest classifier is now clearer.

8.5 Advantages of Decision Trees and Random Forests

The major features of decision trees are simple, easy to visualize and infer results from them. Decision trees work well and provide pretty good results, even on fewer data with lesser degrees of cleaning. They can work well on both numerical and categorical data.

The major features of random forests include employing various decision trees, which carries out attribute selection in a unique way, unaffected by the curse of dimensionality (or to make it simple, the number of features or dimensions), and using a parallel execution to build the random forest. The final predictions are more reliable than from decision trees as random forests use the ensemble model bagging for optimal predictions. This makes the random forest algorithm more stable than the decision tree one.

The major disadvantage of decision trees is that they may overfit quickly, whereas the main disadvantage of random forests is the heavy demand for computational resources.

8.6 Applications of Decision Trees and Random Forests

Both decision trees and random forests may be used for real-time applications in finance, healthcare, customer churn rates, banking sector, e-commerce, stock predictions, prediction of loan repayment by a customer, etc.

8.7 Decision Trees or Random Forest?

Let's first compare them based on certain common factors, as shown in Table 8.1.

The decision to use decision tree or random forest algorithms will completely depend on the real-time problem that you are working on. From the comparison table above, it is clear that, if you need fast prediction, then you should proceed with a decision tree, although the accuracy may be compromised. Hence, it is clear, even though it

Table 8.1 Comparison of Decision Trees and Random Forest

Feature Considered	Decision Tree	Random Forest
How fast the algorithm will work?	Algorithm works faster	Works slow
Ease of Inference	Easy to interpret	It requires expertise otherwise will it is complicated and complex to infer
Time taken	It is faster as only one Decision Tree is generated	Ofcourse , takes more time
How the algorithm responds to Overfitting?	Prone to Overfitting	Overfitting is less because of collection of decision trees.
About the computational resources required?	Less computational resources required	More computational resources required
How about the visualization?	Easy for sure	Complicated
How easy it is to implement?	Fast	Slow
Can we talk about the accuracy?	Accuracy less when compared to Random forest	Accuracy more when compared to Decision Trees

is a time-consuming, computationally expensive, slow process, if you are more focused on the accuracy of the result, you should proceed with the random forest algorithm. As a random forest algorithm uses a collection of decision trees, it might take more time on large datasets, whereas simple decision tree algorithms will work faster on large datasets. If you consider overfitting to be a significant problem, then it would be preferable better to go with random forests than decision trees. Decision trees are easy to visualize and interpret, whereas random forest is more complicated and will be more complex to visualize and interpret as it involves a collection of decision trees and requires more expertise to analyze and interpret.

8.8 Implementation

Let's code to understand the power of optimizations. All these codes are made available in GitHub (https://github.com/shriramkv/MachineLearningwithoneAPI) for the ease of access for the reader. The code is run on the Intel DevCloud and the results are presented for the reader's clearer understanding about how impactful the optimizations are and how powerful oneAPI is. The dataset used is diabetes dataset.

- *Step 1:*

```
import numpy as np
import matplotlib.pyplot as plt
import joblib
import random
import time
```

- *Step 2:* We are going to compare the performance of the stock version of sklearn with the Intel-optimized sklearn. Understand patching is the process which is used to accelerate the process by using optimized versions. This process helps us to understand the added value which the Intel-optimized version brings to the table.

```
from sklearnex import patch_sklearn, unpatch_sklearn

unpatch_sklearn()  # this will set parameters such that the stock version of sklearn will be called
from sklearn import datasets, svm, metrics, preprocessing
from sklearn.ensemble import RandomForestRegressor
from sklearn.model_selection import train_test_split
```

- *Step 3:* Now come the traditional steps. Load the dataset and split it into the training and testing datasets. We ideally keep 80% and 20% of the dataset as the training and testing datasets, respectively. Then, normalization happens as shown below. If the reader is trying this out in DevCloud, it is better to follow the sequence. Remember, the dataset being considered is the diabetes dataset.

```
# Loading the data
digits = datasets.load_diabetes()
X,Y = digits.data, digits.target

# Split dataset into 80% train and 20% test
X_train, X_test, Y_train, Y_test = train_test_split(X, Y, test_size=0.2, shuffle=True)

# normalize the input values by scaling each feature by its maximum absolute value
X_train = preprocessing.maxabs_scale(X_train)
X_test = preprocessing.maxabs_scale(X_test)
```

- *Step 4:* The next step is interesting and here is where the model is created. One can see the stepwise presentation with the comment line, which makes understanding easier. Once this part is executed correctly, the file name where the model is stored will become available. Here, we saved the trained model into a Joblib file. This will help you to use the trained model to use on test or unseen data. This also helps the user to compare the trained model with other contemporary models. Hence, saving the trained model is an important step.

```
# Create a classifier: a support vector classifier
model = RandomForestRegressor()

# Learn on the train subset
fit_st = time.time()
model.fit(X_train, Y_train)
fit_time = fit_st-time.time()

# Save the model to a file
filename = 'finalized_svm_model_unpatch.sav'
joblib.dump(model, filename)

['finalized_svm_model_unpatch.sav']
```

- *Step 5:* Loading the model is the next step, following which the prediction can be made. Also, the time needed for execution is printed to compare the performance of the two variants of sklearn, as mentioned earlier. The time for execution is also printed on the execution.

```
#Loading the model
loaded_model = joblib.load(filename)
t1 = time.time()
#running prediction
Y_pred = loaded_model.predict(X_test)
Regular_RandomForest_time = time.time()-t1
print(Regular_RandomForest_time)

0.007421255111694336
```

The above implementation is with the stock version of sklearn, so now it is time for us to go ahead with the Intel-optimized sklearn. The code will look very similar, with some minor differences.

- *Step 6:* As seen below, this again is the process of importing. But this time it is with the Intel-optimized sklearn that we are going to implement everything. One could get the Intel-optimized version through patch_sklearn(). Once executed, clear indication of the enablement of the Intel-optimized sklearn will appear. The reader can validate the enablement through this message. To recall, patching is used to give that extra boost in the performance, using Intel accelerators.

```
from sklearnex import patch_sklearn, unpatch_sklearn
patch_sklearn()  # this will set parameters such that the optimized version of sklearn will be called
from sklearn import datasets, svm, metrics, preprocessing
from sklearn.ensemble import RandomForestRegressor
from sklearn.model_selection import train_test_split

Intel(R) Extension for Scikit-learn* enabled (https://github.com/intel/scikit-learn-intelex)
```

- *Step 7:* The procedure remains the same here for subsequent steps, as mentioned in the first half of the implementation with the stock version of the sklearn.

```
# digits.data stores flattened ndarray.
digits = datasets.load_diabetes()
X,Y = digits.data, digits.target

# split dataset into 80% train and 20% test
X_train, X_test, Y_train, Y_test = train_test_split(X, Y, test_size=0.2, shuffle=True)

# normalize the input values by scaling each feature by its maximum absolute value
X_train = preprocessing.maxabs_scale(X_train)
X_test = preprocessing.maxabs_scale(X_test)

# Create a randomforest regressor
model = RandomForestRegressor(max_depth = 20,max_leaf_nodes = 5)

# Learn on the train subset
fit_st = time.time()
model.fit(X_train, Y_train)
fit_time = fit_st-time.time()

# Save the model to a file
filename = 'finalized_svm_model_unpatch.sav'
joblib.dump(model, filename)
```

- *Step 8:* Loading the model is followed by the prediction. The time for execution with time for execution is considerably reduced when you use Intel-optimized sklearn (relative to the original version), for the random forest regressor is clearly visible. The increase in the execution speed is presented as a percentage, representing an enormous 898 % of the original. This clearly shows that optimizations are valuable and could certainly provide excellent results.

```
#Loading model
loaded_model = joblib.load(filename)
t1 = time.time()
#running prediction
Y_pred = loaded_model.predict(X_test)
Intel_optimized_RandomForest_time = time.time()-t1
print(time.time()-t1)

0.0006453990936279297

print("percentage increase in speed:",100*(Regular_RandomForest_time - Intel_optimized_RandomForest_time) / I

percentage increase in speed: 898.4599589322382 %
```

It would have definitely been a breezy read, right? Let's move on to ensemble learning and bagging which awaits you in the next chapter, Chapter 9.

Resources

- Vasudevan, S.K., Pulari, S.R., & Vasudevan, S. (2021). Deep Learning: A Comprehensive Guide (1st ed.). Chapman and Hall/CRC. https://doi.org/10.1201/9781003185635
- Murphy, Kevin P., & Bach, F. (2012). Machine Learning: A Probabilistic Perspective. Cambridge, MA, MIT Press.
- https://www.youtube.com/playlist?list=PL3uLubnzL2T1 -7fugIeCk4-l4HVVdn5_v
- https://www.simplilearn.com/tutorials/machine-learning -tutorial/decision-tree-in-python
- https://www.simplilearn.com/tutorials/machine-learning -tutorial/random-forest-algorithm

8.9 Key Points to Remember

1. The decision tree is a supervised learning model.
2. There are two types of decision trees: decision trees for categorical variables (classification) and decision trees for continuous variables (regression).

3. Decision trees help to choose the optimal choice from the leaf nodes.

4. Examples of the various decision Tree algorithms are ID3 (Iterative Dichotomiser 3), CART (Classification and Regression Tree) and C4.5.

5. The major challenge with a decision tree is, "Which attribute should be selected first to achieve that? Or which attribute to select next?" And "Where to perform Attribute split the tree?"

6. Impurity/entropy is the measure of randomness or disorder, or simply it is the uncertainty present in the data.

7. Information gain can be defined as the amount of information gained about a random variable or signal from observing another random variable.

8. Gini Impurity is a method for splitting the nodes when the target variable is categorical.

9. Random forest is an extension of decision trees which contain a group of decision trees, which is applied to the subsets of the dataset.

10. Decision trees and random forest may be used for the real-time applications in finance, healthcare, customer churn rates, banking sector, e-commerce, stock predictions, loan payment prediction by a bank customer, etc.

Quiz Questions (Answer It Yourself, Folks)

1. What are decision trees?
2. List the types of decision trees?
3. What is the major challenge for decision Trees?
4. What are the terminologies entropy and information gain?
5. List the steps involved in a random forest algorithm.
6. Mention the major advantages of decision trees and random forest.
7. List several uses of the applications of decision trees and random forest.
8. How to choose decision trees or random forest for a real-time application?

9
BAGGING

Learning Objectives

After going through this chapter, the reader should be able to understand the following:

- What is ensemble learning?
- Types of ensemble learning.
- What is bagging?
- Why is bagging important?
- Variance and bagging – what's the relationship?
- Major benefits and challenges of bagging.
- Applications of bagging.
- Implementation of bagging.

9.1 Introduction

"Alone, we can do so little; together, we can do so much," the famous saying by Helen Keller is what comes to mind when we talk about ensemble learning. Yes, the ensemble model brings the concept of combining multiple models to improve the predictability of models. This is what we need to understand at the start as bagging, boosting, etc. are the various methods that we use in ensemble modeling. Hence, it is very important to understand what ensemble modeling is before we start digging on bagging.

9.2 What Is Ensemble Learning?

Ensemble methods combine multiple algorithms and are commonly used for regression and classification. These methods are mainly used by those models where they reduce bias and variance to improve the accuracy of the models. They use the concept of base learners. They

DOI: 10.1201/9781003393122-9

incorporate the predictions from all base learners/models to build a more accurate model. Let's consider the case of a brainstorming session, where multiple suggestions might improve the accuracy of the idea being discussed.

In Figure 9.1, it is understood that we consider the dataset and train with various models. Once the training of the model is done, we use a "combiner" to get the best predictions. A single model would be considered as a single base learner, which may not be able to give accurate results due to a high variance or high bias. Hence, multiple single learners are combined, which helps to reduce the bias or variance for producing an optimal model for better performance.

9.3 Types of Ensemble Learning

Ensemble learning is basically divided into homogenous and heterogeneous, where bagging and boosting come under homogeneous ensemble learning techniques, as shown in Figure 9.2. Stacking comes under heterogeneous ensemble learning techniques. Random forest and XGBoost are very well-known and effective homogeneous ensemble learning algorithms used for efficient predictions.

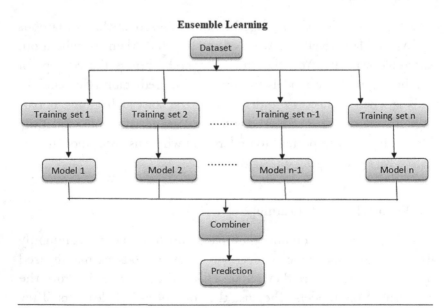

Figure 9.1   Ensemble learning.

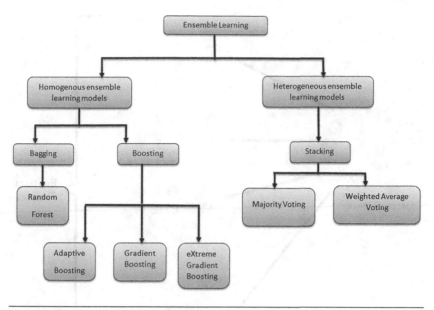

Figure 9.2 Types of ensemble learning.

9.4 What Is Bagging?

Bagging, otherwise known as bootstrap aggregating, is a homogeneous ensemble learning technique. As you know, the aim is to help improve the performance and accuracy of the model to bring about the most optimized prediction model. Bagging has the capability to reduce the bias and variance or, in other words, to deal with a bias–variance trade-off to achieve an optimized prediction model. Hence, it prevents the overfitting of the trained data. Bagging is most commonly used for regression and classification models and works best for decision tree classification algorithms. Now, coming back to the process of bagging, in this technique, the weak or single learners are trained in parallel. Mainly, bagging has three main steps, such as bootstrapping, training done in parallel and aggregation.

9.4.1 Bootstrapping

This is the first step where training samples are randomly generated from the dataset. The same can be visualized in Figure 9.3.

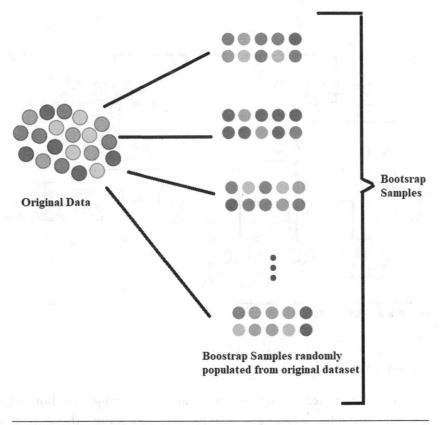

Figure 9.3 Bootstrapping samples.

9.4.2 Aggregation and Optimized Predictions

The bootstrap samples are used with models that work in parallel. They would be aggregated by ensemble models to provide optimized predictions as shown in Figure 9.4.

9.4.3 Steps in Bagging

Bagging is also called bootstrap aggregations. The major steps in bagging are summarized as follows:

1. Bootstrap samples are randomly generated from the original dataset population.
2. A base model is applied to all individual bootstrap samples.
3. Each of the models is learned in parallel with corresponding bootstrap samples individually.

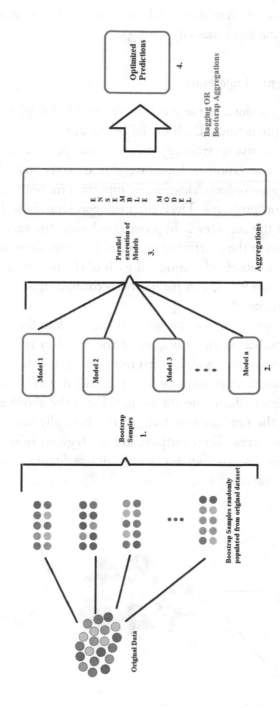

Figure 9.4 Complete bagging process.

4. Optimized predictions are given based on the combined predictions from each of the models (mostly by using a combiner, ensemble model or majority voting).

9.5 Why Is Bagging Important?

Majority voting is done at the combiner/ensemble model to achieve the optimized predictions. Each of the base learners is applied individually to the bootstrap training samples. That is, they are trained independently of one another. Equal weights are given to each model used in the bagging process. Bagging is important for both regression and classification problems. Decision trees commonly use bagging. This is because the accuracy is improved, reducing the variance and thereby eliminating the overfitting problem. Random forest uses bagging, which uses subsets of features in each of the bootstrap samples as shown in Figure 9.5. This topic has been covered in Section 8.4 of this book in Chapter 8.

In the above example, we can see that the random forest ensemble learning method is an extension of the decision tree. Each of the trees gives an output which is fed into the random forest collection. This gives a desired output where the majority of the output is noted. This helps to decide on the output. From the above example, it is clear that the random forest algorithm basically uses a collection of decision trees. Their outputs are aggregated into the final prediction. They have the capability to limit overfitting, thus reducing bias and variance.

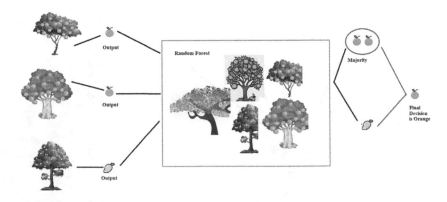

Figure 9.5   Random forest.

9.6 Variance and Bagging – the Major Association

Bagging is mainly used along with decision tree models, which are high-variance models. Bagging works well on such models, compared with low-variance linear regression models. However, compromise on accuracy does happen when bagging is performed on high-bias models. Bagging is used to reduce variance without increasing the bias. That means that a small change in the training set will lead to a large change in the predictions. Bagging uses individual models or base learners with varying means and standard deviation. Then, they are aggregated to get the final predictions. This can only be understood when we try to implement and compare performance with and without bagging, which we will see in the upcoming implementation Section 9.9.

9.7 Major Benefits and Challenges of Bagging

There are many advantages and challenges of bagging. Of these, there are a few worth mentioning. They are summarized as follows:
    The major advantages are,

1. It is easy to implement bagging because of the Python libraries provided by scikit-learn or sklearn. Combining the predictions from multiple base learners to improve the performance of the model is the place where it actually helps.
2. Bagging works well with high-dimensional data. If you have high-dimensional data with lot of missing values, these might lead to high variance, thereby resulting in overfitting and inaccurate predictions as a whole. If bagging is used in such scenarios, it can reduce variance.

The major challenges for bagging include:

1. It is very difficult to infer and interpret the real-time business insights through bagging. This is because of the averaging or combined predictions taken at the end of the bagging process.
2. Bagging involves multiple models and grows more intensive, making it computationally expensive.
3. Bagging methods works well with those algorithms that are less stable, making it less flexible.

9.8 Applications of Bagging

The main applications of bagging include healthcare, the financial industry, fraud detection, credit card frauds, remote sensing, network intrusion detections, bioinformatics, land cover mapping, masonry structures, etc.

9.9 Implementation Example

We are using a wine-quality dataset to implement bagging. Here, with bagging, we are classifying the wine as either red or white. The dataset has chemical indicators and quality metrics with which we can determine the class of the wine. One could have a quick look at how the dataset looks in Figure 9.6.

The implementation is completed, and the code is run on the Intel DevCloud. The code is explained line-by-line and the execution results are also presented below. Also, the code is made available, along with the dataset, in the GitHub: https://github.com/shriramkv /MachineLearningwithoneAPI>

```
# We have considered the wine quality dataset to implement bagging.
# Here with the bagging we are classifying the wine as Red or White.
# The dataset has chemical indicators and quality metrics with which we can determine the class of the wine.
from __future__ import print_function
import os
data_path = ['data']

from sklearnex import patch_sklearn
patch_sklearn()
#unpatch_sklearn()

from io import StringIO
from IPython.display import Image, display
import time

from sklearn.tree import export_graphviz
from sklearn.model_selection import StratifiedShuffleSplit
from sklearn.metrics import mean_squared_error
from sklearn.tree import DecisionTreeRegressor
from sklearn.model_selection import GridSearchCV
from sklearn.metrics import accuracy_score, precision_score, recall_score, f1_score
from sklearn.tree import DecisionTreeClassifier
```

```
Intel(R) Extension for Scikit-learn* enabled (https://github.com/intel/scikit-learn-intelex)
```

```
import pandas as pd
import numpy as np
# Loading data
filepath = 'Wine_Quality_Data.csv'
data = pd.read_csv(filepath, sep=',')
data['color'] = data.color.replace('white',0).replace('red',1).astype(int)
# All data columns except for color
feature_cols = [x for x in data.columns if x not in 'color']
# Split the data into two parts with 1000 points in the test data
# This creates a generator
strat_shuff_split = StratifiedShuffleSplit(n_splits=1, test_size=1000, random_state=42)
# Get the index values from the generator
train_idx, test_idx = next(strat_shuff_split.split(data[feature_cols], data['color']))
# Create the data sets
X_train = data.loc[train_idx, feature_cols]
y_train = data.loc[train_idx, 'color']

X_test = data.loc[test_idx, feature_cols]
y_test = data.loc[test_idx, 'color']

strat_shuff_split.get_n_splits(X_train,y_test)
```

```python
from sklearnex import patch_sklearn, unpatch_sklearn
unpatch_sklearn

from sklearn.ensemble import RandomForestClassifier

# Initialize the random forest estimator
# Note that the number of trees is not setup here
RF = RandomForestClassifier(oob_score=True,
                            random_state=42,
                            warm_start=True,
                            n_jobs=-1)
#out of bag score list
oob_list = list()

# Iterate through all of the possibilities for
# number of trees

for n_trees in [25, 50, 100, 150, 200, 300, 400]:

    # Use this to set the number of trees
    RF.set_params(n_estimators=n_trees)

    # Time fit function
    t = time.process_time()

    # Fit the model
    RF.fit(X_train, y_train)
    elapsed_time = time.process_time() - t

    # Get the oob error
    oob_error = 1 - RF.oob_score_

    # Store it
    oob_list.append(pd.Series({'n_trees': n_trees, 'oob': oob_error}))

rf_oob_df = pd.concat(oob_list, axis=1).T.set_index('n_trees')

print ("It took",elapsed_time," to fit.")
```

```
It took 2.0946468219999996  to fit.
```

```python
from sklearnex import patch_sklearn, unpatch_sklearn
#unpatch_sklearn
patch_sklearn()
from sklearn.ensemble import RandomForestClassifier

# Initialize the random forest estimator
# Note that the number of trees is not setup here
RF = RandomForestClassifier(oob_score=True,
                            random_state=42,
                            warm_start=True,
                            n_jobs=-1)
#out of bag score list
oob_list = list()

# Iterate through all of the possibilities for
# number of trees
for n_trees in [25, 50, 100, 150, 200, 300, 400]:

    # Use this to set the number of trees
    RF.set_params(n_estimators=n_trees)


    # Time fit function
    t = time.process_time()

    # Fit the model
    RF.fit(X_train, y_train)
    elapsed_time = time.process_time() - t

    # Get the oob error
    oob_error = 1 - RF.oob_score_

    # Store it
    oob_list.append(pd.Series({'n_trees': n_trees, 'oob': oob_error}))

rf_oob_df = pd.concat(oob_list, axis=1).T.set_index('n_trees')

print ("It took",elapsed_time," to fit.")

rf_oob_df
```

```python
# We are iterating through number of trees for choosing the hyper parameters and we check 25 trees, 50 trees and
# so on till 400 trees. We found that 150 trees is having the least error and we will be using that as the
# Hyper parameter to do the fit. The time taken for the model to fit is 1.7022535219999995 which is appreciable.
# Again the stock version this is a considerable improvement with 36% reduction in the execution time.
```

```
It took 2.038974479  to fit.
```

	oob
n_trees	
25.0	0.008004
50.0	0.005821
100.0	0.005094
150.0	0.004730
200.0	0.005094
300.0	0.004912
400.0	0.005094

```python
100*(2.069033829999995 - 1.7022535219999995)
# one could see that we have 36% improvement in the performance with the intel optimisation.
```

```
36.67803079999956
```

fixed_acidity	volatile_acidity	citric_acid	residual_sugar	chlorides	free_sulfur_dioxide	total_sulfur_dioxide	density	pH	sulphates	alcohol	quality	color
7.4	0.7	0	1.9	0.076	11	34	0.9978	3.51	0.56	9.4	5	red
7.8	0.88	0	2.6	0.098	25	67	0.9968	3.2	0.68	9.8	5	red
7.8	0.76	0.04	2.3	0.092	15	54	0.997	3.26	0.65	9.8	5	red
11.2	0.28	0.56	1.9	0.075	17	60	0.998	3.16	0.58	9.8	6	red
7.4	0.7	0	1.9	0.076	11	34	0.9978	3.51	0.56	9.4	5	red
7.4	0.66	0	1.8	0.075	13	40	0.9978	3.51	0.56	9.4	5	red
7.9	0.6	0.06	1.6	0.069	15	59	0.9964	3.3	0.46	9.4	5	red
7.3	0.65	0	1.2	0.065	15	21	0.9946	3.39	0.47	10	7	red
7.8	0.58	0.02	2	0.073	9	18	0.9968	3.36	0.57	9.5	7	red
7.5	0.5	0.36	6.1	0.071	17	102	0.9978	3.35	0.8	10.5	5	red
6.7	0.58	0.08	1.8	0.097	15	65	0.9959	3.28	0.54	9.2	5	red
7.5	0.5	0.36	6.1	0.071	17	102	0.9978	3.35	0.8	10.5	5	red
5.6	0.615	0	1.6	0.089	16	59	0.9943	3.58	0.52	9.9	5	red
7.8	0.61	0.29	1.6	0.114	9	29	0.9974	3.26	1.56	9.1	5	red
8.9	0.62	0.18	3.8	0.176	52	145	0.9986	3.16	0.88	9.2	5	red
8.9	0.62	0.19	3.9	0.17	51	148	0.9986	3.17	0.93	9.2	5	red
8.5	0.28	0.56	1.8	0.092	35	103	0.9969	3.3	0.75	10.5	7	red
8.1	0.56	0.28	1.7	0.368	16	56	0.9968	3.11	1.28	9.3	5	red
7.4	0.59	0.08	4.4	0.086	6	29	0.9974	3.38	0.5	9	4	red
7.9	0.32	0.51	1.8	0.341	17	56	0.9969	3.04	1.08	9.2	6	red
8.9	0.22	0.48	1.8	0.077	29	60	0.9968	3.39	0.53	9.4	6	red
7.6	0.39	0.31	2.3	0.082	23	71	0.9982	3.52	0.65	9.7	5	red
7.9	0.43	0.21	1.6	0.106	10	37	0.9966	3.17	0.91	9.5	5	red
8.5	0.49	0.11	2.3	0.084	9	67	0.9968	3.17	0.53	9.4	5	red
6.9	0.4	0.14	2.4	0.085	21	40	0.9968	3.43	0.63	9.7	6	red
6.3	0.39	0.16	1.4	0.08	11	23	0.9955	3.34	0.56	9.3	5	red
7.6	0.41	0.24	1.8	0.08	4	11	0.9962	3.28	0.59	9.5	5	red

Figure 9.6   The wine-quality dataset.

We hope you found that this chapter was also interesting. To complete this field, the concepts of boosting and stacking await you in Chapter 10. Let's progress to that next chapter.

Resources

- Vasudevan, S.K., Pulari, S.R., & Vasudevan, S. (2021). Deep Learning: A Comprehensive Guide (1st ed.). Chapman and Hall/CRC. https://doi.org/10.1201/9781003185635.
- Murphy, K. P. & Bach, F. (2012) Machine Learning: A Probabilistic Perspective. Cambridge, MA, MIT Press.
- https://www.youtube.com/playlist?list=PL3uLubnzL2Tl-7fugIeCk4-14HVVdn5_v
- https://www.simplilearn.com/tutorials/machine-learning-tutorial/bagging-in-machine-learning
- https://www.geeksforgeeks.org/bagging-vs-boosting-in-machine-learning/
- https://www.javatpoint.com/bias-and-variance-in-machine-learning

9.10 Key Points to Remember

1. The ensemble model brings the concept of combining multiple models to improve the predictability of models.
2. Ensemble methods are commonly used for regression and classification.
3. Ensemble learning is basically divided into homogeneous or heterogeneous.
4. Bagging, otherwise known as bootstrap aggregating, is a homogeneous ensemble technique.
5. Bagging has the capability to reduce bias and variance for an optimized prediction model.
6. Bagging has three steps, mainly bootstrapping, parallel training and aggregations.
7. Bagging is used to reduce variance without increasing bias.
8. Bagging is easy to implement and can work well with high-dimensional data.

9. Bagging is less flexible and it is very difficult to interpret the insights.
10. Random forest uses bagging and is an extension of the bagging technique.
11. Bagging is computationally expensive.
12. Healthcare, the financial industry, fraud detection, credit card frauds, remote sensing, network intrusion detections, bioinformatics, land cover mapping, masonry structures, etc. are specific areas of research where bagging is used.
13. Bagging can prevent overfitting by reducing the bias and variance trade-off.

    The following points are taken from the article: https://www.javatpoint.com/bias-and-variance-in-machine-learning and found useful to improve understanding.
14. High bias/low variance (underfitting): predictions are consistent, but inaccurate on average. This can happen when the model uses very few parameters.
15. High bias/high variance: predictions are inconsistent and inaccurate on average.
16. Low bias/low variance: it is an ideal model, but we cannot achieve this.
17. Low bias/high variance (overfitting): predictions are inconsistent and accurate on average. This can happen when the model uses a large number of parameters.

Quiz Questions (Answer It Yourself, Folks)

1. What is ensemble learning?
2. List the types of ensemble learning.
3. What is bagging?
4. What are the major steps involved in bagging?
5. Why is bagging important?
6. What is the major relationship between bagging and variance?
7. State the major applications of Bagging.
8. Can you elaborate on the advantages of bagging?
9. Can you explain the major disadvantages of bagging?
10. List a few applications of bagging.

10

Boosting and Stacking

Learning Objectives

After reading this chapter, the reader should be able to understand the following:

- What is boosting?
- Types of boosting algorithms.
- Why is boosting important?
- Bias and boosting – what's the association?
- Comparison of bagging and boosting.
- Major applications of boosting.
- Major benefits and challenges of boosting.
- What is stacking?
- Types of stacking algorithms
- Why is stacking important?
- Implementation of stacking

10.1 Introduction

Ensemble methods use multiple models and a combiner at the end to decide about the accurate prediction methods suitable for the data being used. Yes, there are bagging, boosting and stacking methods available and we have seen in detail about the bagging method in Chapter 9. In this chapter, we are going to explore more about the other two techniques of ensemble learning, that is boosting and stacking. We will also do a proper comparison between bagging and boosting methods in this chapter. By the end of this chapter, you will have a complete idea about why we use ensemble learning methods in machine learning and their importance. Let's get started.

DOI: 10.1201/9781003393122-10

10.2 What Is Boosting?

Boosting is an ensemble learning technique that uses sequential ways of using the base learners rather than the parallel way of using multiple base learners, as in bagging. I know, it seems to be a bit vague as of now. Let's try to understand it in depth. Say you have developed a model which can identify tigers. Your model has been trained to identify tigers. Now, the issue is that the model is trained only with tiger images but, at times, it misclassifies the domestic cat as a tiger.

However, our model has to accurately classify only tigers. Yes, the tiger belongs to the cat family, ☺ we agree. But we need a specific tiger classification system, maybe we are building a system to identify the tigers that enter the nearby neighborhood, thereby causing panic among the humans therein. In such cases, if we misclassify a fully grown cat from a distance, our system fails, as shown in Figure 10.1. Here, boosting comes to the rescue by training multiple models, but in a sequential manner, to improve the accuracy of the model on unseen data. So, now you know where boosting can be utilized.

The sequential process followed in boosting can be best understood from Figure 10.2.

The major steps in the boosting process, as shown in Figure 10.2, are as follows:

It is good to understand that this process is a generic one and that the training process changes based on the boosting algorithm used.

Anyway, moving on to the process:

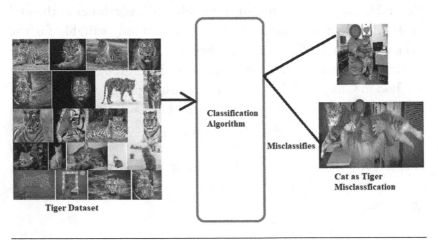

Tiger Dataset

Classification Algorithm

Misclassifies

Cat as Tiger
Misclassfication

Figure 10.1   Misclassification.

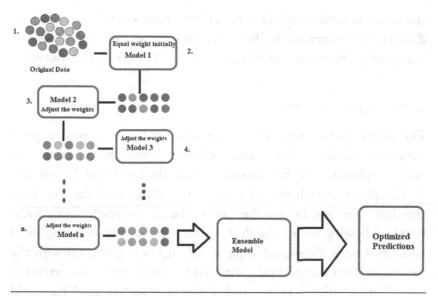

Figure 10.2 Boosting process.

1. Equal weights are assigned to each of the original data samples and are fed to the first model in the boosting algorithm. At this stage, it makes predictions for each data sample. Normally, they are referred to as base algorithms. So, basically, the base algorithm predicts each data sample in the original dataset.
2. The boosting algorithm assigns weight, based on the model performance, that increases the weight of samples with a more significant error. There are many models and the model with the optimized predictions will contribute more to the final predictions.
3. This continues and the weights are adjusted at each model.
4. Steps 2 and 3 continue until the training errors are less than a minimum threshold value.

The final predictions are used for inferring interpretations for the applications. In the boosting process, if you notice, it uses a sequential process for proceeding through the algorithm. This is different from the parallel process of execution followed in the bagging process.

10.3 Types of Boosting Algorithms

Now, let's explore the various types of boosting algorithms. Exploring each one in detail is beyond the scope of this book. However, it is very important to understand the types of algorithm and to know the basic differences between them. The three main types are adaptive boosting, gradient boosting and eXtreme Gradient boosting (XGBoost).

10.3.1 *Adaptive Boosting*

One of the first models that was created for boosting was adaptive boosting (AdaBoost). Every time the boosting procedure is repeated, it adjusts and makes an effort to self-correct. The initial weight assigned by AdaBoost to each dataset is the same. After each decision tree, the data point weights are then automatically adjusted. To fix them for the following round, the decision tree applies adjusted weights to those that were improperly categorized. It keeps going through the procedure until the residual error, that is, the difference between the actual and predicted values, falls below a predetermined threshold value (Figure 10.3).

AdaBoost is versatile and generally less sensitive than other boosting algorithms. It may be used with a wide variety of predictors.

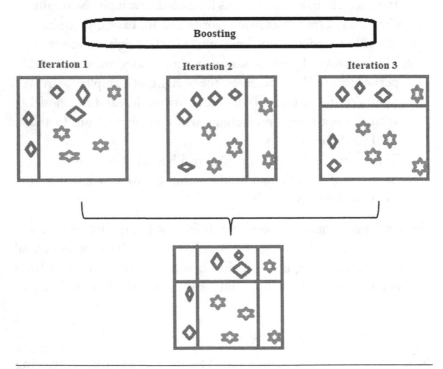

Figure 10.3   AdaBoost.

When features are correlated or if the data are highly dimensional, this method does not perform well.

10.3.2 Gradient Boosting

Gradient boosting doesn't adjust the weights as in AdaBoost. Instead, it uses a differential loss function which uses the difference between the predicted values and ground truth. Gradient boosting also uses the sequential training model. This boosting process makes sure that the current base learner/model is better than the previous ones. This method normally delivers accurate measures at the initial steps itself (Figure 10.4).

10.3.3 Extreme Gradient Boosting (XGBoost)

In numerous ways, Extreme Gradient Boosting (XGBoost), as illustrated in Figure 10.5, enhances gradient boosting in terms of computational speed and scaling. To enable parallel learning during training, XGBoost makes use of the CPU's multiple cores. Big data applications find this boosting approach interesting since it can handle massive datasets. Parallelization, distributed computing, cache optimization, non-linearity, cross-validation, scalability and out-of-core processing are some of the XGBoost standout characteristics. Explaining each of these is beyond the scope of this book, although parallelizing the whole boosting process improves the training time and the algorithm tends to always produce optimized predictions.

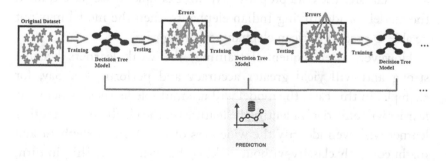

Figure 10.4 Gradient boosting.

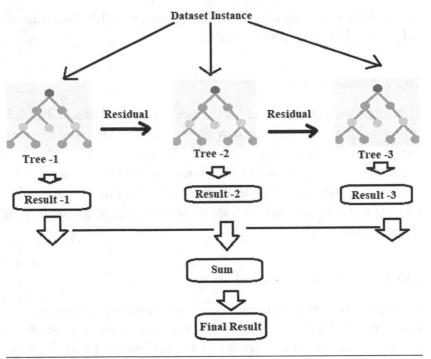

Figure 10.5   XGBoost.

10.4 Why Is Boosting Important?

Like bagging, boosting is also an important ensemble technique which uses the sequential training model to strengthen the weak base learners more with each step than the previous one. This creates a strong learner which will give accurate predictions, thereby improving the performance of the model. Base learners initially will have low accuracy for prediction and are susceptible to overfitting, and won't be able to classify the data properly. Say, for example, if we have trained the model for identifying Indian elephants, then the model may not be able to predict African elephants with big ears.

However, after sequential training, the weak learners become strong and will yield greater accuracy and performance. Say, for example, in this case, the model will use multiple learners, where one learner will effectively identify the features of the elephant and another learner will even identify the wide ears of the African elephant and might correctly classify without making the system fail. This, in turn, will improve the accuracy and performance of the system.

10.5 Bias and Boosting

The weak learners are converted into strong learners in the boosting process. The models will have high bias and low variance. The boosting process is helpful for models with underfitting, as shown in Figure 10.6.

In the underfitting, we could clearly see how badly the learner fits the data points. It is best shown when a learner or model is used to show the residual errors. The data points that are incorrectly categorized would be assigned higher weights. This is actually a way to deal with the errors or residuals. As every time a new stronger learner/model is introduced, it will start making better predictions on the data observations and start correcting the misclassified predictions in the best way possible by the model. This will eventually reduce the errors and give optimized predictions, making the model a strong learner for the scenario. This is how bias and boosting are connected. However, boosting is good for regression and classification problems.

10.6 Major Applications of Boosting

Boosting is widely used in many real-time applications where regression and classification come into the picture. AdaBoost algorithms are widely used for customer churn (percentage of customers lost by a business in a given time period) prediction and categorizing the types of interests of customers in the market. Applications of the XGBoost algorithm involve regression, classification, ranking and diverse prediction problems.

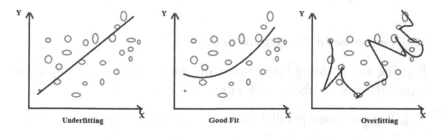

Figure 10.6 Various fitting scenarios.

10.7 Major Benefits and Challenges of Boosting

Boosting has many benefits and challenges, depending on the type of boosting algorithm, the dataset, the amount of missing and sparse data, etc. However, here we will quote the generic benefits and challenges of boosting algorithms.

The major benefits are as follows:

1. Boosting algorithms are supposed to be easily understandable and hence easy to interpret. They learn from either a parallel or sequential weak base learner and make it strong by serial iterations by increasing the weights based on the errors. This helps to reduce high bias.
2. Boosting algorithms have the capability to handle missing data and don't require pre-processing.
3. Boosting algorithms can handle large datasets and aim to identify important features by increasing the predictive accuracy during training, which increases the computational efficiency of the algorithm.
4. Boosting can very well prevent overfitting. The XGBoost algorithm is widely used for major regression and classification problems as they can work independently of small, medium and large datasets.

The major challenges include:

1. Boosting algorithms are very sensitive to outliers, which will result in a skewed distribution.
2. XGBoost algorithms are not good for very sparse data.
3. Boosting algorithms are not that scalable and tend to be highly complex when compared with other methods, thus making it challenging for them to be used in real-time applications.

10.8 Comparison of Bagging and Boosting

Bagging and boosting have major differences in the processing techniques they use, as shown in Figure 10.7.

1. Bagging uses parallel execution of base learners, whereas boosting uses sequential execution of base learners

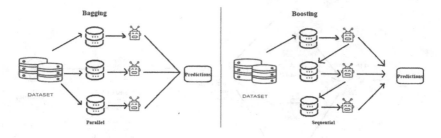

Figure 10.7 Bagging and boosting.

2. Individual models are fed with data samples separately in bagging, whereas, in boosting, each new model formed is based and improved on the previous model built.
3. Bagging reduces variance and boosting helps to reduce high bias and variance.
4. Bagging may reduce overfitting better than boosting algorithms.
5. Bagging uses the average of n learners for the final prediction, whereas boosting uses the weighted average of n learners for the final prediction.
6. In bagging, each model receives equal weight, whereas, in the boosting process, the model receives weights according to performance.

10.9 What Is Stacking?

Now, as we have studied bagging and boosting ensemble methods, it's time for us to understand the stacking ensemble method, which is shown in Figure 10.8.

Stacking, also called stacked generalization, is an ensemble model which uses multiple models to explore different parts of the problem, rather than the whole of the problem as such. The theme is to use intermediate models to make predictions and then use a new model which uses these intermediate predictions for achieving the best prediction. That is why this model is called stacking as the final prediction model is built, or stacked, on top of other models. This stacking model is supposed to give better predictions than the individual model predictions.

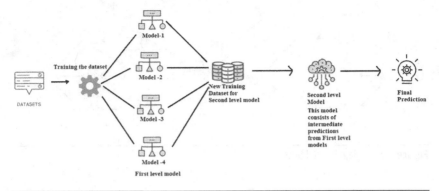

Figure 10.8   Stacking.

The steps in the stacking process are as follows:

1. Similar to k-fold cross-validation, we divided the training dataset into k-folds.
2. On the k-1 parts, a base model is fitted, and predictions are given for the kth part.
3. We repeat the same for each section of the training dataset.
4. After that, the base model is fitted to the entire training dataset to determine how well it performs on the test set.
5. For various base models, we repeat the previous three steps.
6. The features of the second-level model are drawn from predictions made by the training dataset.
7. The prediction is made using a second-level model on the test dataset.

Blending is a kind of stacking that uses validation and a test dataset for the whole process to make predictions.

10.10 Types of Stacking Algorithms

The stacking algorithms are mainly divided into majority voting and weighted average ensemble models.

10.10.1 Majority Voting

Say, we take an example of sentiment analysis, which we all know. Consider the sentence "It is shining bright and I feel happy. I think I should call my friends and plan a trip" as shown in Figure 10.9. This

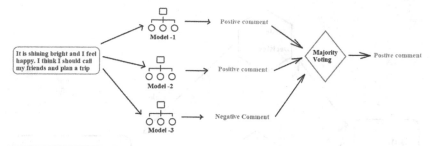

Figure 10.9 Majority voting.

is the sentence given for you to identify whether it is positive, negative or neutral.

Let's apply this sentence to multiple classifiers or models. Each of the models has predicted different sentiments say, model-1 predicted it to be positive, model-2 to be positive again and model-3 to be negative. Then, these results are passed through a majority voting model, where the model identifies the majority positive sentiment and gives a prediction of positive sentiment for our input sentence. Simple statistics are used to get the final prediction, e.g., mean or median in the majority voting ensemble methods.

10.10.2 Weighted Average Ensemble

This is a variant of the majority voting ensemble, which uses a diverse collection of multiple models. This method finds the average weight of each member in the training dataset, based on their performance. To make an impact, it finds the weight of each member based on the performance on the validation set using k-fold cross-validation. It also uses optimization algorithms to fine-tune the hyperparameters for weights assigned for each model for best performance, as shown in Figure 10.10.

The weighted average ensemble uses the weighted average of prediction from each member separately.

10.10.3 Why Is Stacking Important?

The major benefit of stacking is that it uses a diverse set of optimized models for predictions. Stacking is highly suitable for classification and regression tasks.

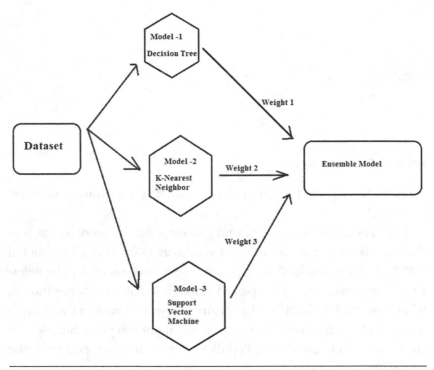

Figure 10.10 Weighted average ensemble.

10.11 XGBoost Implementation

The piece of code presented below shows the way we will be predicting prices of houses in California based on the features of each house, using Intel optimizations for XGBoost shipped as a part of the oneAPI AI Analytics Toolkit. It starts with importing the necessary modules and libraries as shown below.

```
import xgboost as xgb
from sklearn.metrics import mean_squared_error
from sklearn.datasets import fetch_california_housing
from sklearn.model_selection import train_test_split
from sklearn.metrics import r2_score
import pandas as pd
import numpy as np
```

```
#Loading the data
california = fetch_california_housing()
#converting data into a pandas dataframe
data = pd.DataFrame(california.data)
data.columns = california.feature_names

#setting price as value to be predicted, This is what to be predicted
#(You will get only one colomn as output and that is price)
data['PRICE'] = california.target

#extracting rows, we slice.
X, y = data.iloc[:,:-1],data.iloc[:,-1]

#using dmatrix values for xgboost
#DMatrix is an internal data structure that is used by XGBoost which is optimized for both memory efficiency
#You can construct DMatrix from multiple different sources of data.
#XGBoost uses CART(Classification and Regression Trees) Decision trees.
data_dmatrix = xgb.DMatrix(data=X,label=y)

#splitting data
X_train, X_test, y_train, y_test = train_test_split(X, y, test_size=0.25, random_state=1693)
#The random state hyperparameter in the train_test_split() function controls the shuffling process.
```

Next, instantiate and define the XGBoost regression object by calling the XGBRegressor() class from the library and the same is presented in the screenshot that follows.

Terminology of XGBoost

- *Learning rate*: This simply means how fast the model learns. If the learning rate is very fast, we will skip the optimal solution. If it is too slow, we will need too many iterations to converge to the best values. So, using a good learning rate is crucial.
- *Maximum depth of a tree*: Increasing this value will make the model more complex and more likely to overfit. XGBoost aggressively consumes memory when training a deep tree!
- *colsample_bytree*: This is a family of parameters for the subsampling of columns. All colsample_by* parameters have a range of [0, 1], the default value being 1, and specify the fraction of columns to be subsampled. colsample_bytree is the subsample ratio of columns when constructing each tree. Subsampling occurs once for every tree constructed.
- *ALPHA*: The L1 regularization term on weights. Increasing this value will make the model more conservative: default =1; combats overfitting.
- *n_estimators*: the number of runs XGBoost will try to learn. This is the number of trees you want to build before taking the maximum voting or averages of predictions. Higher number of trees gives you a better performance but makes your code slower.

- *tree_method string [default= auto]*: The tree construction algorithm used in XGBoost.
- *Hist*: A faster histogram optimized to approximate to greedy algorithm.

```
xg_reg = xgb.XGBRegressor(objective ='reg:squarederror', colsample_bytree = 0.3, learning_rate = 0.1,
                          max_depth = 5, alpha = 10, n_estimators = 10, tree_method='hist')
# Model without training.
print (xg_reg)
```

```
XGBRegressor(alpha=10, base_score=None, booster=None, colsample_bylevel=None,
             colsample_bynode=None, colsample_bytree=0.3, gamma=None,
             gpu_id=None, importance_type='gain', interaction_constraints=None,
             learning_rate=0.1, max_delta_step=None, max_depth=5,
             min_child_weight=None, missing=nan, monotone_constraints=None,
             n_estimators=10, n_jobs=None, num_parallel_tree=None,
             random_state=None, reg_alpha=None, reg_lambda=None,
             scale_pos_weight=None, subsample=None, tree_method='hist',
             validate_parameters=None, verbosity=None)
```

What next? Simple, the fitting and training model comes next.

```
xg_reg.fit(X_train,y_train) # Trained model
# we train our model, with our data.
preds = xg_reg.predict(X_test)
# Trained model is to be tested with the test dataset.
print(X_test)
print(preds) # price here!
```

```
       MedInc  HouseAge  AveRooms  AveBedrms  Population  AveOccup  Latitude  \
8111   2.7183      48.0  3.905380   1.098330      1807.0  3.352505     33.79
379    2.4962      37.0  5.324324   1.108108       835.0  3.223938     37.75
18071  9.1569      22.0  7.252669   0.925267       773.0  2.750890     37.28
4462   4.9231       8.0  4.748936   1.136170       435.0  1.851064     34.10
6077   4.5100      22.0  5.858597   1.067873      2315.0  2.618778     34.10
...       ...       ...       ...        ...         ...       ...       ...
6354   2.5275      27.0  4.246654   1.036329      1328.0  2.539197     34.14
14797  2.3253      14.0  4.239732   1.088852      3662.0  3.069573     32.57
9718   3.3472      37.0  6.625000   1.015625       266.0  4.156250     36.87
14789  2.3603      27.0  4.071839   1.071839       814.0  2.339080     32.58
1595   6.8686      35.0  6.666667   1.053030       352.0  2.666667     37.89

       Longitude
8111     -118.20
379      -122.17
18071    -122.01
4462     -118.18
6077     -117.85
...          ...
6354     -117.96
14797    -117.10
9718     -121.77
14789    -117.13
```

```
rmse = np.sqrt(mean_squared_error(y_test, preds))
print("RMSE:",rmse)
# Accuracy for the model built is being found, We are evaluating the model.
# Lower values of RMSE indicate better fit.
# RMSE is a good measure of how accurately the model predicts the response

RMSE: 1.0823382872176526
```

One can save the results now and export the same to the csv file.

```
pd.DataFrame(preds).to_csv('foo.csv',index=False)
```

```
print("[CODE_SAMPLE_COMPLETED_SUCCESFULLY]")
[CODE_SAMPLE_COMPLETED_SUCCESFULLY]
```

One could see the results in the csv file, foo.csv.

A portion of the obtained results is presented here as shown in Figure 10.11.

Well, this is the end of the chapter! Let's navigate to the next chapter to learn about Clustering Techniques and Principal Component Analysis.

1	1.3631656
2	1.2941495
3	2.162086
4	1.6937927
5	1.6418169
6	1.6923952
7	1.6800449
8	1.4700606
9	1.3147323
10	1.6449367
11	0.96372133
12	1.5471326
13	1.354381
14	1.441846
15	1.5426086

Figure 10.11 Result displayed as CSV file.

Resources

- Vasudevan, S.K., Pulari, S.R., & Vasudevan, S. (2021). Deep Learning: A Comprehensive Guide (1st ed.). Chapman and Hall/CRC. https://doi.org/10.1201/9781003185635.
- Murphy, K.P., & Bach, F. (2012). Machine Learning: A Probabilistic Perspective. Cambridge, MA, MIT Press.

- https://www.youtube.com/playlist?list=PL3uLubnzL2Tl -7fugIeCk4-l4HVVdn5_v
- https://www.javatpoint.com/stacking-in-machine-learning
- https://www.geeksforgeeks.org/stacking-in-machine -learning/

10.12 Key Points to Remember

1. Boosting is an ensemble learning technique which uses a sequential way of using the base learners to create a strong learner for optimized predictions.
2. Adaptive boosting, gradient boosting and XGBoost are types of boosting algorithms.
3. The boosting process is helpful for models with underfitting.
4. AdaBoost algorithms are widely used for customer churn pre-diction and categorizing the types of interests of customers in the market.
5. Applications of the XGBoost algorithm involve regression, classification, ranking and diverse prediction problems.
6. Boosting algorithms are used for regression and classification tasks.
7. Bagging may reduce overfitting better than boosting algorithms.
8. Stacking, also called stacked generalization, is an ensemble model which uses multiple models to explore different parts of the problem but not the whole of the problem as such.
9. The stacking algorithms are mainly categorized into majority voting and weighted average ensemble models.
10. Stacking is very well suited for classification and regression tasks.

Quiz Questions (Answer It Yourself, Folks)

1. What is boosting?
2. What are the types of boosting algorithms used in machine learning?
3. List the major applications of boosting algorithms.
4. Compare bagging and boosting algorithms in detail.

5. What is stacking?
6. List the major types of stacking algorithms.
7. Why is stacking important?

11

CLUSTERING TECHNIQUES AND PRINCIPAL COMPONENT ANALYSIS

Learning Objectives

After reading this chapter, the reader should be able to understand the following:

- K-means clustering
- Implementation of K-means clustering
- Curse of dimensionality
- Principal component analysis (PCA)
- Implementation of PCA

11.1 Introduction

To make it simple, clustering is a method or technique which groups data into clusters. The objects inside a cluster should have high similarity. For example, in a dataset of medical students, first-year students represent a cluster, second-year students are a cluster, etc. The objects in one cluster should be different from those in another cluster; for example, first-year engineering students are one cluster that is dissimilar to a second cluster of first-year medical students. These two clusters are disjoint. Clustering helps to divide the complete dataset into many clusters. This is a non-labeled, unsupervised approach. One can understand clustering by referring to Figure 11.1.

It is time to understand K-means clustering.

 DOI: 10.1201/9781003393122-11

Cluster – A (Medical Students – I
Year)

Cluster – B (Engineering Students
– I Year)

Figure 11.1   Clustering.

11.2 K-Means Clustering

As discussed before, clustering is a method or technique to group data into clusters with the objects inside the cluster possessing greater similarity than the objects in another cluster. A cluster's objects should be markedly dissimilar to the objects from another cluster. In one word, we can say that the metric being employed is "similarity!" It is the metric which talks about the relationship between the objects.

Now comes the next question: Why do we need clustering? Simple, it gives you an exploratory view of the data. One can get a better idea about the data with clustering.

K-means is actually called "centroid-based clustering." "What is a centroid?" is the next question to be answered! The dictionary definition is that a centroid is the center of mass of a geometric object of uniform density. Well, in ML, the centroid definition remains the same. It is the data point at the center of a cluster.

The centroid need not be a member of the dataset considered, though it can be.

This clustering approach is iterative in nature. This means that the algorithm keeps working until the target is achieved. One sample dataset is taken and clustering is explained step by step.

The challenge in this example is to group the eight objects in the dataset into two clusters. All the objects have the X, Y and Z coordinates clearly accessible. How do we identify the K value? K is the number of clusters. Here, it is two. So, in this example, the K value is set as 2.

Can we have a look at the dataset? (see Table 11.1)

Initially, we must take any two centroids, C1 and C2. Next question: why select just two centroids? Since the K value is 2, the number of centroids chosen is also 2. Once chosen, the data points get tagged

Table 11.1   Dataset Considered for Clustering

OBJECTS	X	Y	Z
01	1	4	1
02	1	2	2
03	1	4	2
04	2	1	2
05	1	1	1
06	2	4	2
07	1	1	2
08	2	1	1

to a particular cluster based on the distance. It is time to start with the computation:

- First centroid = object 2 (O2); this will be cluster 1 (O2 = first centroid = 1, 2, 2)
- Second centroid = O6; this will be cluster 2 (O6 = second centroid = 2, 4, 2)

Can we choose any object as the centroid? This is a very common question – any object can become a centroid.

How do we measure distance? There is a formula, which comes to our rescue here.

- $d=|x2-x1|+|y2-y1|+|z2-z1|$

People call d the Manhattan distance.

- d is the distance between two objects.
- Remember – any object has X, Y and Z coordinates according to the dataset! So, the task is simple.

It is time to reconstruct the table and one must use the distance between each object and the centroids chosen (see Table 11.2).

Like O1, O2 and O3, the rest of the calculations are carried out to compute the distance from C1 and C2. One can refer to Table 11.2 to get a clearer understanding.

The next step is to go ahead with the clustering. How is it achieved? Simple! Based on the distance, one can go ahead with the clustering. Whichever is shorter – say C1 is shorter than C2 – for an object, the object falls to C1. Hence, the clustering shall look like:

Table 11.2 Distance from C1 and C2

OBJECTS	X	Y	Z	DISTANCE FROM C1 (1,2,2)	DISTANCE FROM C2 (2,4,2)
O1	1	4	1	D= |1−1|+|4−2|+|2−1|= 3	D= |1−1|+|4−2|+|2−1|=2
O2	1	2	2	D= |1−1|+|2−2|+|2−2|=0	D= |2−1|+|4−2|+|2−2|= 3
O3	1	4	2	D= |1−1|+|4−2|+|2−2|=2	D= |2−1|+|4−4|+|2−2|=1
O4	2	1	2	2	3
O5	1	1	1	2	5
O6	2	4	2	3	0
O7	1	1	2	1	4
O8	2	1	1	3	4

For a clear understanding, the following color guidelines have been followed in Table 11.3. Cluster 1 is represented in green and cluster 2 in red.

To clarify, one can refer to Table 11.4 as presented below.

- Cluster 1: ((1+2+1+1+2)/5, (2+1+1+1+1)/5,(2+2+1+2+1)/5) = (1.4,1.2,1.6)
- Cluster 2: ((1+1+2)/3, (4+4+4)/3, (1+2+2)/3) = (1.33, 4, 1.66).

The next round (iteration) of clustering then has to be done (see Table 11.5).

Now, the new clusters will be:

Cluster 1
O2
O4
O5
O7
O8

Cluster 2
O1
O3
O6

So, we can stop here. No updates in the centroids or changes in the cluster grouping have been observed. Hence, this is the correct clustering.

This is how K-means clustering works.

One can listen to the lecture on K-Means clustering by the authors at the video link at https://youtu.be/Fuq9Dw43co0

11.3 Implementation of K-Means Clustering

K-means clustering has been carried out on the mall dataset, where we have variables on the customers such as age, gender, annual

Table 11.3   Clustering – the Next Level

Cluster 1
OB-2 (0 < 3)
OB-4 (2 < 3)
OB-5 (2 < 5)
OB-7 (1 < 4)
OB-8 (3 < 4)

Cluster 2
OB-1 (3 >2)
OB-3 (2 >1)
OB-6 (3 >0)

Objects	X	Y	Z	Distance from C1(1,2,2)	Distance from C2(2,4,2)
01	1	4	1	D= |1-1|+|4-2|+|2-1|= 3	D= |1-1|+|4-2|+|2-1|=2
02	1	2	2	D= |1-1|+|2-2|+|2-2|=0	D= |2-1|+|4-2|+|2-2|= 3
03	1	4	2	D= |1-1|+|4-2|+|2-2|=2	D= |2-1|+|4-4|+|2-2|=1
04	2	1	2	2	3
05	1	1	1	2	5
06	2	4	2	3	0
07	1	1	2	1	4
08	2	1	1	3	4

Table 11.4   Clusters 1 and 2

Objects	X	Y	Z
01	1	4	1
02	1	2	2
03	1	4	2
04	2	1	2
05	1	1	1
06	2	4	2
07	1	1	2
08	2	1	1

income and spending ability. Based on these entries, our model will be classifying the customers. For the reader to understand what the dataset looks like, a sample screenshot of the dataset is presented in Figure 11.2.

With the Intel oneAPI and the optimized associated libraries, it becomes easy for software developers to build solutions. One can read through the code below code, step by step, to understand how the implementation has been done effortlessly. The code is also made available in the GitHub with the dataset at: https://github.com/shri-ramkv/MachineLearningwithoneAPI.

Table 11.5   Reiterated Results

Objects	X	Y	Z	Distance from C1(1.4,1.2,1.6)	Distance from C2(1.33, 4, 1.66)
O1	1	4	1	3.8 (1.4 -1 + 4 − 1.2 + 1.6 -1)	1 (1.33 − 1 + 4 − 4 + 1.66 − 1)
O2	1	2	2	1.6 (1.4- 1+ 2 − 1.2 + 2 − 1.6)	2.66 (1.33 − 1+ 4 − 2 + 2 − 1.66)
O3	1	4	2	3.6	0.66
O4	2	1	2	1.2	4
O5	1	1	1	1.2	4
O6	2	4	2	3.8	1
O7	1	1	2	1	3.66
O8	2	1	1	1.4	4.33

	CustomerID	Genre	Age	Annual Income (k$)	Spending Score (1-100)
1	0001	Male	19	15	39
2	0002	Male	21	15	81
3	0003	Female	20	16	6
4	0004	Female	23	16	77
5	0005	Female	31	17	40
6	0006	Female	22	17	76
7	0007	Female	35	18	6
8	0008	Female	23	18	94
9	0009	Male	64	19	3
10	0010	Female	30	19	72
11	0011	Male	67	19	14
12	0012	Female	35	19	99
13	0013	Female	58	20	15
14	0014	Female	24	20	77
15	0015	Male	37	20	13
16	0016	Male	22	20	79
17	0017	Female	35	21	35

Figure 11.2   Mall dataset – a quick reference.

```
# K-Means Clustering
# Here, the K-Means clustering has been implemented with oneAPI to cluster the customers for a mall considered
# based on Age, Gender, Annual Income, and spending ability.

from sklearnex import unpatch_sklearn
unpatch_sklearn()
# unpatching lets you use the stock version of SKLearn.

# Importing the libraries
import numpy as np
import matplotlib.pyplot as plt
import pandas as pd
import time

# Importing the dataset
dataset = pd.read_csv('Mall_Customers.csv')
X = dataset.iloc[:, [3, 4]].values


# Using the elbow method to find the optimal number of clusters.
# Refer to the graph to understand the concept (One should see between 4 and 6, least sharp bend,
# which denotes the errors inturn the clusters are decided)

from sklearn.cluster import KMeans
wcss = []
for i in range(1, 11):
    kmeans = KMeans(n_clusters = i, init = 'k-means++', random_state = 42)
    kmeans.fit(X)
    wcss.append(kmeans.inertia_)
plt.plot(range(1, 11), wcss)
plt.title('The Elbow Method')
plt.xlabel('Number of clusters')
plt.ylabel('WCSS')
plt.show()


# Fitting K-Means to the dataset
kmeans = KMeans(n_clusters = 5)
y_kmeans = kmeans.fit_predict(X)

# Visualising the clusters
plt.scatter(X[y_kmeans == 0, 0], X[y_kmeans == 0, 1], s = 100, c = 'red', label = 'Cluster 1')
plt.scatter(X[y_kmeans == 1, 0], X[y_kmeans == 1, 1], s = 100, c = 'blue', label = 'Cluster 2')
plt.scatter(X[y_kmeans == 2, 0], X[y_kmeans == 2, 1], s = 100, c = 'green', label = 'Cluster 3')
plt.scatter(X[y_kmeans == 3, 0], X[y_kmeans == 3, 1], s = 100, c = 'cyan', label = 'Cluster 4')
plt.scatter(X[y_kmeans == 4, 0], X[y_kmeans == 4, 1], s = 100, c = 'magenta', label = 'Cluster 5')
plt.scatter(kmeans.cluster_centers_[:, 0], kmeans.cluster_centers_[:, 1], s = 300, c = 'yellow', label = 'Centroids')
plt.title('Clusters of customers')
plt.xlabel('Annual Income (k$)')
plt.ylabel('Spending Score (1-100)')
plt.legend()
plt.show()
```

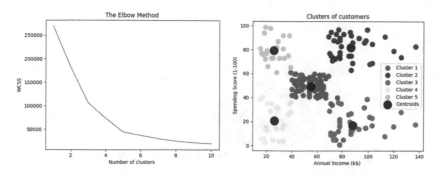

Figure 11.3 The clusters.

One can visualize the clusters from the results obtained below (see Figure 11.3).

11.4 Principal Component Analysis (PCA)

Now that we know the complete working of the K-means clustering algorithm, let's move on to understanding one of the most important concepts in machine learning, principal component analysis (PCA).

Have you heard about the Curse of Dimensionality? Yes, I am talking about a curse ☺. Let's try to understand, with an example, what this is and how is it relevant to the topic that we are talking about!

Consider you are a zoophile, a lover of animals. Say that you are so fond of animals that you live in a forest area (in a treehouse) so that you can enjoy the animals in their natural habitat, rather than caging them.

One day, while enjoying nature and trekking over a mountain, you find a beautiful snail moving over a tree trunk. You get yourself lost in enjoying the snail moving in one direction (one-dimensional movement) (see Figure 11.4).

Next, you are distracted by a pack of pups, running around in a distant field plane (two-dimensional movement). Even though you are happy to enjoy the sight, fear strikes as you realize that they are not puppies but fox cubs ☺ and you resume trekking (see Figure 11.5).

Finally, you reach the top of the mountain, and lay down looking at the blue sky, enjoying the birds fly (three-dimensional movement) (see Figure 11.6).

Figure 11.4   One-dimensional movement.

Figure 11.5   Two-dimensional movement.

Figure 11.6   Three-dimensional movement.

So, you enjoy the sunset and start back to your treehouse! Say, on your way back, you encounter some energy beings (aka ghosts ☺), then of course you have even encountered a higher-dimensional being (Figure 11.7).

Figure 11.7 Higher-dimensional movement.

However, to cut a long story short, you scare the ghost and it disappears. Hurray! You reach your treehouse safe and sound ☺.

Now, let's connect this small story to our concept of the "Curse of Dimensionality." It's very simple. Just imagine, if you are trying to catch a snail which moves in one dimension, of course this would have been the easiest task. However, if you are trying to catch the pups running in two dimensions, yes, you could have done that, of course but it is not such an easy task as catching the snail. Then, just imagine, you are a hunter trying to catch the birds flying in three dimensions; oh my God, only that hunter knows the pain. Finally, if you are trying to catch the ghost, our higher-dimensional being, of course, that would be the toughest job of all.

What are we trying to conclude here? Yes, it is simple. As the number of dimensions increases, things become more and more complicated to deal with. Yes, you know now ☺.

Let's make it more technical! In our problems, we use datasets. Consider that there is a huge dataset which contains a large number of attributes; the number of attributes indirectly provides information about the dimensionality of the dataset space. Normally, for humans, it is not that easy to visualize any dimensions greater than 3. So, is there a way that we can reduce the number of attributes (features) in a dataset? However, when we reduce the attributes, the predominant thing to be kept in mind is that this reduction should not lose any valuable information or relationships among the data in the dataset. The principal component analysis is a widely used dimensionality reduction method which makes use of an excellent exploratory data analysis tool to understand the variations in the dataset in a beautiful manner.

11.5 PCA in Depth

We will start where we left off. Principal component analysis is a dimensionality reduction method that figures out the correlations and patterns in a dataset, so that when the data are reduced to a lower dimension, all the important information related to attributes and their relationships is preserved.

When reducing the higher dimension to a lower dimension, PCA eliminates the inconsistencies and removes the redundant data and highly correlated features as shown in Figure 11.8. Why the highly correlated features? In a dataset, if you have two attributes which are highly correlated to each other or, in other words, if the correlation coefficient is close to 1, that means that the strength of the relationship is high. In such cases, if you retain one of the attributes and remove the other, it will not make any difference to your final result as you are able to preserve the information and relationship, with the help of one attribute alone.

Consider there a crowd attending a function, as shown in Figure 11.9. You, being the photographer for the function, need to capture the best photo of the crowd. Hence, you need to identify the

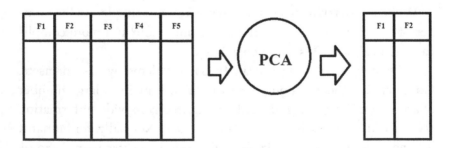

Figure 11.8   Simplest representation of PCA.

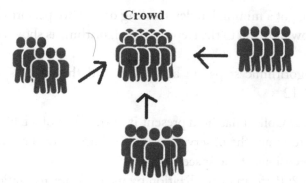

Crowds from different directions and positions

Figure 11.9 Crowd from different positions.

direction and position you need to fix the camera and lighting, so that the maximum number of people in the crowd are included in the photos taken for the event.

When mapping them all onto a straight line, considering three straight lines (projections) for three positions as shown in Figure 11.10, it is understood that the greatest number of people from the crowd is actually covered in line 3. This means that the projection on straight line 3 is better than on the other projections, 1 and 2. Why? It is because line 3 preserves more information than the other projections.

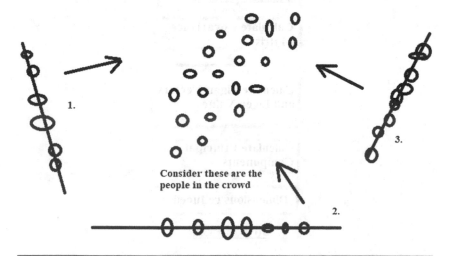

Figure 11.10 How a crowd is mapped to three straight lines from three positions?

Having got a minimal understanding of how we perform PCA, we should now move on to the steps in the algorithm, as shown in Figure 11.11.

The algorithmic steps are as follows and the same is shown in Figure 11.12.

- *Step 1:* Collect data and present it in the form of a table where the rows are the observations and columns are the attributes (dimensions of the space).
- *Step 2:* Perform normalization by using Z-normalization

$$\mathbf{Z} = (\mathbf{X} - \mathbf{M}) / \mathbf{S}$$

where m is the mean, and S is the standard deviation.

- *Step 3:* Calculate the covariance matrix.
- *Step 4:* Calculate the eigenvectors and eigenvalues. Make sure that the eigenvectors are unit vectors (have a length of 1).
- *Step 5:* Inspect the eigenvalues and select the eigenvector with the highest eigenvalue, which determines the *first principal*

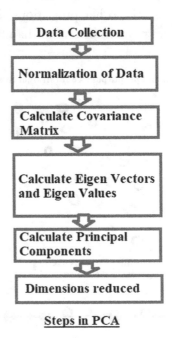

Steps in PCA

Figure 11.11   Steps in PCA.

To refresh Eigen Vectors and Eigen Values

Consider this example,

$$\begin{pmatrix} 4 & 6 \\ 4 & 1 \end{pmatrix} \times \begin{pmatrix} 1 \\ 3 \end{pmatrix} = \begin{pmatrix} 22 \\ 7 \end{pmatrix}$$

$$\begin{pmatrix} 4 & 6 \\ 4 & 2 \end{pmatrix} \times \begin{pmatrix} 3 \\ 2 \end{pmatrix} = \begin{pmatrix} 24 \\ 16 \end{pmatrix} = 8 \times \begin{pmatrix} 3 \\ 2 \end{pmatrix}$$

- **Eigenvectors**

  In the first example, the resulting matrix, a vector, is not an integer multiple of the original vector, while in the second example it is 8 times vector of the original one.

Please note:

  - The vector $\begin{pmatrix} 3 \\ 2 \end{pmatrix}$ is the eigenvector. It is a vector that

  points to a the point (3, 2) in the coordinate system.

Now to understand about Eigen Values:

Eigenvalues

- Eigenvalues are multiples of eigenvectors. In our example, the value of 8 is the eigenvalue associated to the eigenvector.
- Eigenvectors and eigenvalues always come in pairs. An eigenvector is a **direction** and the eigenvalue is a **magnitude** of the eigenvector.

Figure 11.12   Understanding eigenvectors.

component (it preserves the greatest percentage of the information from the dataset). The eigenvector with the next highest eigenvalue determines the *second principal component* and so on. We can ignore the eigenvectors with a low eigenvalue: this leads to dimensionality reduction.

- *Step 6:* Reconstruct the *data into a new dataset.* For the selected eigenvector/eigenvectors, create a transpose matrix and multiply it from the left by the adjusted dataset matrix.

Resulting Data = (Eigenvector Matrix)^T × Adjusted Data Matrix

Some major points to be kept in mind include:

- If your data set is of *9 dimensions, then 9 principal components are computed,* such that, *the first principal component* stores the *maximum information possible* and the *second one* stores the remaining maximum information and so on.
- For every eigenvector, there is an eigenvalue.
- The number of attributes in the data determine the number of eigenvectors that is to be calculated.

We hope you have understood the process of principal component analysis and how the principal components are calculated in order to reduce the dimensions of the dataset without causing the loss of relevant and important information. See Figure 11.13 for a complete understanding of PCA from 5D to 2D.

11.6 Implementation of PCA

To demonstrate how powerful oneAPI could be in implementing the PCA, the following piece of code and demonstrations are presented. We have considered the famous IRIS dataset for the dimensionality reduction. One could visualize the dataset from Figure 11.14. Also, the performance of the Intel distribution of sklearn is compared with the stock sklearn, and you can try this out as well.

```
# Here, with the PCA we load the IRIS data set, and try to reduce the dimensions.
# Ideally, 4 is getting reduced to 2 dimensions.
import pandas as pd
import numpy as np
import matplotlib.pyplot as plt
from sklearn.decomposition import PCA
from sklearn.preprocessing import StandardScaler
%matplotlib inline
import time
# We have done all the neccessary importing, here.
```

```
Intel(R) Extension for Scikit-learn* enabled (https://github.com/intel/scikit-learn-intelex)
```

One could see that the stock version is used first, followed by the Intel-optimized version.

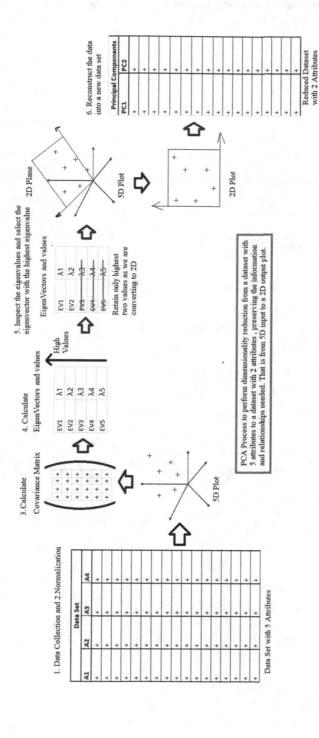

Figure 11.13 The complete process of PCA from 5D to 2D.

Id	SepalLengthCm	SepalWidthCm	PetalLengthCm	PetalWidthCm	Species
1	5.1	3.5	1.4	0.2	Iris-setosa
2	4.9	3	1.4	0.2	Iris-setosa
3	4.7	3.2	1.3	0.2	Iris-setosa
4	4.6	3.1	1.5	0.2	Iris-setosa
5	5	3.6	1.4	0.2	Iris-setosa
6	5.4	3.9	1.7	0.4	Iris-setosa
7	4.6	3.4	1.4	0.3	Iris-setosa
8	5	3.4	1.5	0.2	Iris-setosa
9	4.4	2.9	1.4	0.2	Iris-setosa
10	4.9	3.1	1.5	0.1	Iris-setosa
11	5.4	3.7	1.5	0.2	Iris-setosa
12	4.8	3.4	1.6	0.2	Iris-setosa
13	4.8	3	1.4	0.1	Iris-setosa
14	4.3	3	1.1	0.1	Iris-setosa

Figure 11.14   The IRIS dataset.

```
# using stock version
from sklearnex import unpatch_sklearn
unpatch_sklearn()
from sklearn.decomposition import PCA
# Loading dataset into Pandas DataFrame
url = "https://archive.ics.uci.edu/ml/machine-learning-databases/iris/iris.data"
df = pd.read_csv(url
                , names=['sepal length','sepal width','petal length','petal width','target'])
#defining features and target
features = ['sepal length', 'sepal width', 'petal length', 'petal width']
x = df.loc[:, features].values
y = df.loc[:,['target']].values
# performing feature scaling
x = StandardScaler().fit_transform(x)
```

```
#running PCA
t1 = time.time()
pca = PCA(n_components=2)
principalComponents = pca.fit_transform(x)
t2 = time.time()

# storing result as dataframe
principalDf = pd.DataFrame(data = principalComponents
            , columns = ['principal component 1', 'principal component 2'])
finalDf = pd.concat([principalDf, df[['target']]], axis = 1)
print(t2-t1)
```

```
0.40245604515075684
```

```
from sklearnex import patch_sklearn
patch_sklearn()
from sklearn.decomposition import PCA

# Loading dataset into Pandas DataFrame
url = "https://archive.ics.uci.edu/ml/machine-learning-databases/iris/iris.data"
df = pd.read_csv(url
                , names=['sepal length','sepal width','petal length','petal width','target'])
#defining features and target
features = ['sepal length', 'sepal width', 'petal length', 'petal width']
x = df.loc[:, features].values
y = df.loc[:,['target']].values
# performing feature scaling
x = StandardScaler().fit_transform(x)
```

```
#running PCA
t1 = time.time()
pca = PCA(n_components=2)
principalComponents = pca.fit_transform(x)
t2 = time.time()

# storing result as dataframe
principalDf = pd.DataFrame(data = principalComponents
              , columns = ['principal component 1', 'principal component 2'])
finalDf = pd.concat([principalDf, df[['target']]], axis = 1)
print(t2-t1)
```

```
0.0016429424285888672
```

```
Intel(R) Extension for Scikit-learn* enabled (https://github.com/intel/scikit-learn-intelex)
```

```
100*(0.40245604515075684 - 0.0016429424285888672)
# This confirms we get a 40% improvement in the performance with the intel optimized sklearn.
```

```
40.0813102722168
```

One can see the swift increase in performance with the Intel-optimized sklearn over the stock version. The complete code and dataset is made available in the GitHub: https://github.com/shri-ramkv/MachineLearningwithoneAPI and the reader can try this out.

We sincerely hope you had a great read. It's almost curtains now, but not before we describe the additional Intel tools that can provide you with an enhanced development experience! Let's move on to the last chapter. Chapter 12 awaits you.

Resources

- Vasudevan, S.K., Pulari, S.R., & Vasudevan, S. (2021). Deep Learning: A Comprehensive Guide (1st ed.). Chapman and Hall/CRC Press. https://doi.org/10.1201/9781003185635
- Murphy, K.P., & Bach, F. (2012). Machine Learning: A Probabilistic Perspective. Cambridge, MA, MIT Press.
- https://youtu.be/n7npKX5zIWI
- https://youtu.be/7G4UW4qkfOs

11.7 Key Points to Remember

1. Clustering is a method or technique to group data into clusters. The objects inside a cluster should have a high similarity.
2. K-means is determined by a technique known as "centroid-based clustering." A centroid is the center of mass of a

geometric object of uniform density. The centroid definition remains the same in machine learning.

3. With the Intel oneAPI and the optimized libraries all around, it becomes easy for developers to build solutions for clustering problems.

4. Intel-optimized sklearn is more effective and powerful than the stock sklearn.

5. The Curse of Dimensionality says that, as the number of dimensions increases, things becoming more and more complicated to deal with.

6. Principal component analysis is a widely used dimensionality reduction method which uses an excellent exploratory data analysis tool to understand the variations in the dataset in a beautiful manner.

Quiz Questions (Answer It Yourself, Folks)

1. What is K-means clustering?
2. What is the Curse of Dimensionality?
3. What is principal component analysis?
4. List the major steps involved in PCA.
5. Try all the codes presented in the GitHub link and see if you are able to confirm the performance improvements.

12

MORE Intel TOOLS FOR ENHANCED DEVELOPMENT EXPERIENCE

Learning Objectives

After reading this chapter, the reader should be able to understand the following:

- How Intel distribution for Python is different.
- How to install and use Intel distribution for Python.
- What is Intel OpenVINO?
- How to use OpenVINO.

12.1 Intel Distribution for Python

The Intel Distribution for Python (a cluster of packages) improves the speed of common libraries and algorithms, especially data analytics, to yield better performance. The new optimization provides significant speedups for scikit-learn (a free software machine learning library). especially in NumPy (short for Numerical Python) and SciPy (Scientific Python) packages meant for performing various operations with the data. It also leverages Intel Data Analytics Acceleration Library (Intel DAAL). The performance speed can be seen to accelerate around a whopping 140 times for several scikit-learn algorithms. Intel DAAL is a software development library that is highly optimized for Intel architecture processors and provides building blocks for all data analytics stages, from data preparation to data mining and machine learning.

The Intel Distribution for Python includes accelerated packages for NumPy, SciPy and scikit-learn (or sklearn) that are drop-in compatible with other similar community packages. Since these accelerated

DOI: 10.1201/9781003393122-12   **181**

packages best utilize the Intel hardware already available, no code changes are needed.

The readers can visit intel.com/content/www/us/en/developer/tools/oneapi/distribution-for-python.html#gs.3ou56q to download the Intel Distribution for Python.

As a first step to install and use the Intel Distribution for Python, one has the option to go ahead with Intel AI Analytics Toolkit or via Anaconda.

We will choose the option of Anaconda and the following steps need to be done, in sequence.

As shown in Figure 12.1 below, one must click the Anaconda Prompt.

Next, one needs to update conda with the command "conda update conda". One will receive the "status completion" message on correct execution (see Figure 12.2).

Add the Intel channel as the next step. One needs to inform conda to choose the Intel packages rather than the default packages, when available, by issuing the command "conda config --add channels intel" (see Figure 12.3).

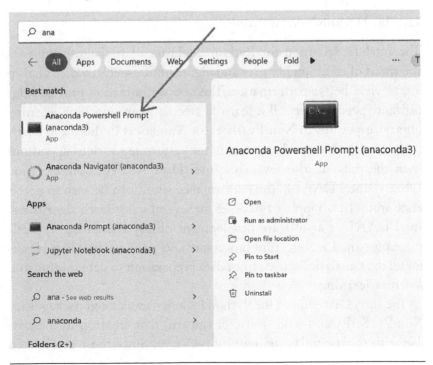

Figure 12.1   Anaconda Prompt.

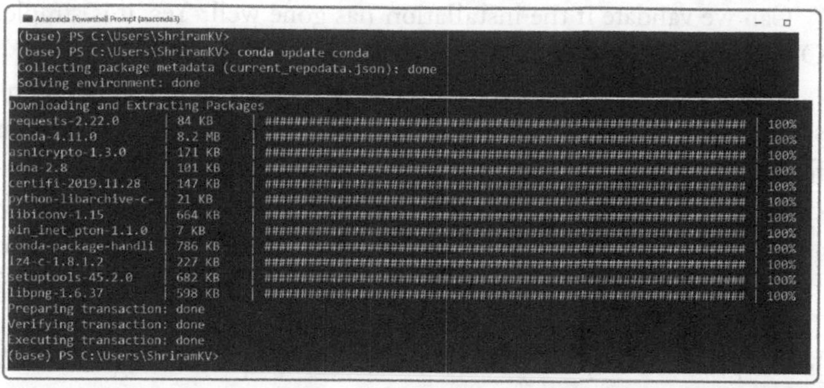

Figure 12.2   Conda update screen.

```
(base) PS C:\Users\ShriramKV> conda config --add channels intel
```

Figure 12.3   Add Intel channel.

As the next step, install Intel Distribution for Python via conda. It is recommended that you create a new environment when installing. To install the core python3 environment, issue the command "conda create -n idp intelpython3_core python=3.x". One can refer to the below screenshot to understanding the process (Figure 12.4).

Please note that "x" in "python=3.x" should signify which version of Python you would like to install.

Finally, activate the Conda environment (Figure 12.5).

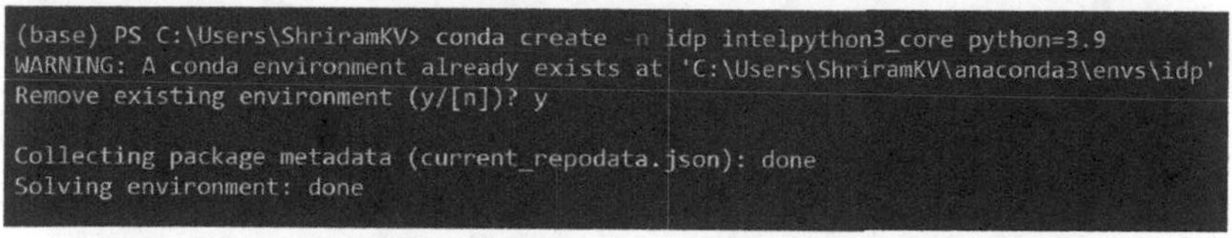

```
(base) PS C:\Users\ShriramKV> conda create -n idp intelpython3_core python=3.9
WARNING: A conda environment already exists at 'C:\Users\ShriramKV\anaconda3\envs\idp'
Remove existing environment (y/[n])? y

Collecting package metadata (current_repodata.json): done
Solving environment: done
```

Figure 12.4   Installation of Intel Python.

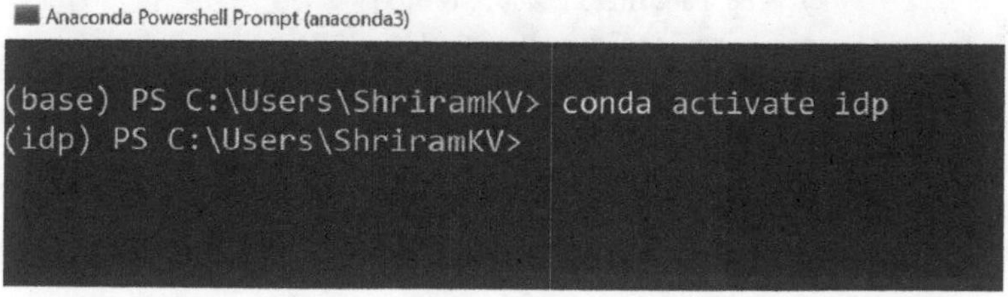

```
Anaconda Powershell Prompt (anaconda3)

(base) PS C:\Users\ShriramKV> conda activate idp
(idp) PS C:\Users\ShriramKV>
```

Figure 12.5   Activate Conda.

Can we validate if the installation has gone well? Yes, it is simple. One should refer to Figure 12.6 to know how to do this.

Below is a piece of sample code (Figure 12.7) to be taken into consideration to run with the stock version Python and Intel Distribution for Python. Once executed, we should note the time needed for execution of each of the Python variants (Figure 12.8).

To understand the difference, the Intel Distribution brings to the table, the same piece of code has been executed with the Intel Distribution for Python. One could see that there is a good difference in the performance, with Intel Distribution outperforming the stock version (Figure 12.9).

One can use Intel Distribution for Python to get better results and certainly this has been agreed by developers all over the world. It is time for us to learn the Intel OpenVINO.

Figure 12.6   Validation.

```
import numpy as np
import time

start = time.time()

rd = np.random.RandomState(88)
a = rd.randint(1,1000,(1000,1000))
y = rd.randint(1,1000,(1000))
res = np.linalg.solve(a,y)

end = time.time()

print(res)
print('Time Consuming:',end-start)
```

Figure 12.7   Sample code.

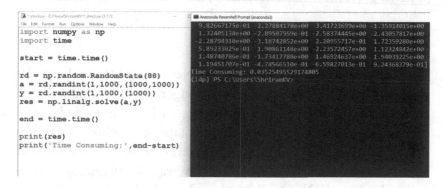

Figure 12.8 Time consumed with stock version Python.

Figure 12.9 Time consumed with Intel Python.

12.2 What Is OpenVINO?

OpenVINO (Open Visual Inference and Neural Network Optimization) is a cross-platform deep learning toolkit developed by Intel. It focuses on optimizing neural network inference with a write-once, deploy-anywhere approach for Intel hardware platforms. The toolkit is free for use and has two versions: OpenVINO toolkit, which is supported by the open-source community, and the Intel Distribution of OpenVINO toolkit, which is supported by Intel. By using the OpenVINO toolkit, software developers can select models and deploy pre-trained deep learning models (YOLO v3, ResNet 50, etc.) through a high-level C++ Inference Engine API integrated with application logic. A pre-trained model denotes a model created by someone and trained on a large dataset to solve a similar problem that can be used as a starting point, instead of building a model from scratch.

YOLOv3 (You Only Look Once, Version 3) is a real-time object detection algorithm that identifies specific objects in videos, live feeds or images. The YOLO machine learning algorithm makes use of the features learned by a deep CNN (Convolutional Neural Network) for object detection. ResNet, which stands for Residual Network, is a specific type of CNN and is generally used to power computer vision applications. ResNet-50 is a CNN that is 50 layers deep, and it achieves greater accuracy.

OpenVINO provides integrated functionalities for accelerating the development of applications and solutions that solve several tasks, using computer vision, automatic speech recognition, natural language processing, recommendation systems, machine learning and more.

12.2.1 Why Use OpenVINO?

The recent advances in Deep Neural Networks (DNNs) have elevated the accuracy of computer vision algorithms to a higher level. Nevertheless, deploying and producing such accurate and useful models need adaptations for the computational methods as well as the hardware. OpenVINO allows optimization of the DNN model to be a streamlined, efficient process by way of integrating various tools. The OpenVINO toolkit is based on the latest generations of Artificial Neural Networks (ANN), such as CNN, as well as recurrent and attention-based networks.

The OpenVINO toolkit maximizes the performance and accelerates application development by employing a library of predetermined functions, as well as pre-optimized kernels. Also, the other computer vision tools, such as OpenCV (Open Source Computer Vision Library), OpenCL Kernels etc., are included in the OpenVINO toolkit. OpenCL™ (Open Computing Language) is a low-level API for heterogeneous computing that runs on GPUs.

12.2.2 Benefits of OpenVINO

The benefits include:

- Accelerating performance by enabling simple execution methods across different Intel processors and accelerators, such as CPU, GPU/Intel Processor Graphics, VPU (Vector Processing unit) and FPGA.

- Streamlining Deep Learning (DL) deployment by way of providing one centralized method for implementing dozens of DL models.
- Customizing DL model layers without the burden of framework overheads, implementing parallel programming of various accelerators.
- Allowing users to extend artificial intelligence (AI) within private applications.
- Optimizing AI all the way to the cloud with processes such as the Model Optimizer, Intermediate Representation, nGraph Integration and more.
- nGraph Library is an open-source C++ library and runtime / compiler suite for DL networks. This facilitates usage of preferred deep learning frameworks on any number of hardware architectures, for both training and inference.

12.2.3 What Is the Recent Version?

The recent version is the 2022.3 LTS (Long-Term Support) and it comes with excellent features. This makes it very easy for developers to innovate. The new release powers developers with more performance-oriented developments, many deeper learning models, enhanced device portability and, more importantly, improved inferencing performance with very limited code changes.

The recent version provides the developers with:

a. Broader Model and Hardware Support.
b. Expanded Model Coverage.
c. Improved API and More Integrations.

OpenVINO is cool and one can understand the cycle of innovation with OpenVINO clearly by referring to Figure 12.10.

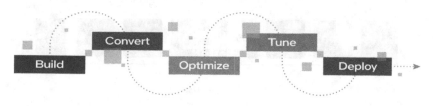

Figure 12.10 OpenVINO cycle of innovation.

OpenVINO has become so popular and is so celebrated because of its ability to convert and optimize models with such frameworks as TensorFlow, PyTorch or Caffe. Also, the deployment becomes easier as it can be done across a mix of Intel hardware as well as environments. One can also deploy on-premises, on-device or in the cloud, making it so flexible for developers to choose the best they wish to use. Fig. 12.11 presents you with a clear view of how much more powerful and flexible OpenVINO is.

One can see that it can be either a CPU, GPU, VPU or FPGA. That's an amazing convenience which the developer receives.

12.2.4 How to Install?

One needs to understand that the OpenVINO installation package is distributed in two parts: OpenVINO Runtime and OpenVINO Development Tools. It is recommended to install these two in one go instead of just installing the OpenVINO Runtime.

What is OpenVINO Runtime? It includes a set of libraries for running machine learning model inference on the processors. What are the Development Tools? They are the utilities that help working with the OpenVINO and OpenVINO models. The tools include

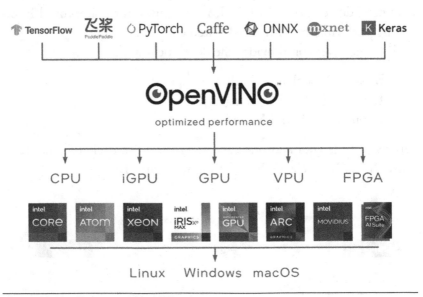

Figure 12.11   The power of OpenVINO.

the Model Optimizer, Benchmarking Tool, Accuracy Checker and Annotation Converter.

One can follow the guidelines and instructions available @ https://docs.openvino.ai/2022.2/openvino_docs_install_guides_overview .html for a smooth installation.

12.2.5 Resources Link?

The first thought which hits the mind of developers with any new platform or tool is, "Do I have resources to make the learning and practice easier?" The reply is a strong YES with the OpenVINO.

One would fall in love with the tutorials crafted and presented in the link @ https://docs.openvino.ai/2022.2/tutorials.html

Developers get free hands to the Jupyter Notebooks, and the tutorials are presented in a very easy way for smooth, flawless learning and practice.

One could see that the examples are presented with the link to launch the notebook with ease. This is a fine feature which makes life of learners much easier.

On clicking the launch button (see Figure 12.12), immediately one can see that the Binder gets launched in the browser as shown in Figure 12.13. No installations or anything else is required to run these sample codes with this approach. It may take a few minutes to

First steps with OpenVINO

Brief tutorials that demonstrate how to use Python API for inference in OpenVINO.

Notebook	Description	Preview
001-hello-world launch binder	Classify an image with OpenVINO.	
002-openvino-api launch binder	Learn the OpenVINO Python API.	OpenVINO
003-hello-segmentation launch binder	Semantic segmentation with OpenVINO.	
004-hello-detection launch binder	Text detection with OpenVINO.	

Figure 12.12   Sample codes and Demo0073.

Figure 12.13   The Binder launch.

launch the Jupyter Notebook. One can take a look at the log messages if the delay seems more than expected to understand what's happening.

Notebooks with a Binder button can be run without installing anything. Once you have found the tutorial of your choice, just click the button next to the name of it and Binder will start it in a new tab of the browser. Binder is a free online service with limited resources.

Once launched, the screen, as seen in Figure 12.14, with the sample code chosen (in this case, it is an image classification tutorial), will be opened in the Jupyter NBViewer and can be explored further. One can even download the notebook as required.

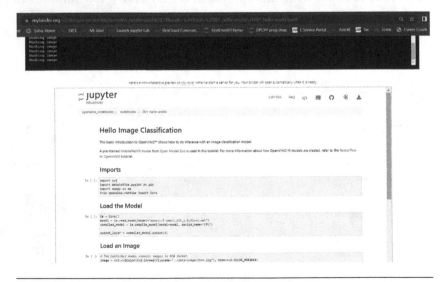

Figure 12.14   Jupyter Notebook – image classification example.

That's it! We have come to the end of this book. We are certain that it was an enjoyable ride of learning!

12.2.6 *Key Points to Remember*

- Intel Distribution for Python is an optimized Python version and provides results superior to the stock Python version.
- After installation of the Intel Distribution for Python, one should confirm whether the installation is effective and can be done with command: python.
- OpenVINO (Open Visual Inference and Neural Network Optimization) is a cross-platform deep learning toolkit developed by Intel.
- Currently, the most recent OpenVINO version is the 2022.3 LTS and it comes with excellent features, which make it very easy for developers to innovate.
- OpenVINO has become so popular and celebrated because of its ability to convert and optimize models with frameworks as TensorFlow, PyTorch or Caffe.
- One can also deploy on-premises, on-device or in the cloud which reflects the flexibility offered by OpenVINO.
- All of the OpenVINO tutorials are outlined @ https://docs .openvino.ai/2022.2/tutorials.html.
- The sample codes and tutorials can be launched through the Binder and developers can run the Jupyter Notebook as required.

Exercises

1. Write any complex piece of code and try running the code with the stock Python and the Intel Distribution for Python. What's the inference?
2. Install Intel Distribution of OpenVINO. Try running the sample codes.

Index

Printed in the United States
by Baker & Taylor Publisher Services

Printed in the United States
by Baker & Taylor Publisher Services